Anti Gravity Device Company

Library of Congress Control Number 2017903178

ISBN-13: 978-0-692-85379-5

Anti Gravity Device Company:

Or,

How To Build a Skateboard Ramp

...you might need a crane.

A public online photo album illustrating these stories has been created and at this printing is being maintained at:

www.antigravitydevicecompany.com

For Kingston

Cover Photo: Jamie Johnston on the Taj Mah Wall

CONTENTS

Thanks to my nephew Adam Khan for his encouragement, advice and expert proofreading.

Photo albums illustrating parts of the story can be found free online at:

Antigravitydevicecompany.com

Roll In

In my universe, there's a lottery of rare adventures: worthy building projects with a circus of skilled and quirky cohorts. I have a peculiar kind of luck. I get to be one of the builders. The world of construction is my amusement park.

The simple fact that I need a job or a project to survive faces me with an urgent puzzle at each turn of the wheel, and I'm sure that's one of my luck charms. I've got to have a gig. The material question has always been a ticket to adventure for me. My son Johnny (JW) has been another source of good fortune. He grew up on Hawaii's Big Island, and when he was high school age, we moved to the mainland. We had four years together in Southern California before he would be on his own. We opened doors for each other, climbed over fences, or crawled under gates, ignored "no trespassing" signs. We set out to have a good time, and hit the jackpot.

People want something built for lots of different reasons. Projects over the years have sprung out necessity, or art, or profit; out of luxury and vanity, or comfort. I find satisfaction in the things we've built and I find fun in the daily exchanges between the crews, clients, inspectors and contractors. In the case of building skateboard ramps, where the whole motivation is fun, it has been doubly satisfying and triple the fun, since my co-workers were skaters themselves, a famously fun-loving subculture. For these few years, it was my pleasure to apply my skills to the crafting of ideal surfaces for their kinetic sensual pastime.

I started work at Powell-Peralta Skateboards in Santa Barbara, California in 1987 just in time to take part in the building of a mobile halfpipe that toured the country with our professional team for years. From that time on, I was in the middle of the company's ramp building efforts, making many small ramps used for our public demos and contests, becoming progressively more elaborate, leading up to the creation of the SkateZone indoor skatepark at the company factory in 1990.

We became close friends with the key players of the R&D department and skaters who worked at the company and travelled with them to some of the top skateboard parks and locations on the West Coast, from Tijuana to Vancouver. Our unofficial R&D mission was learning as much as we could about ramp building so that when we finally got to build the SkateZone, we would know what it was that made the good ones good, the fun ones fun, and the dangerous ones dangerous. All the time, I was taking pictures, and JW was making drawings.

In 1991, with the SkateZone completed, and JW living over by SB City College, I moved on to Northern California to continue my carpenter's odyssey, thinking

I was leaving the skateboard world behind. In 1997, to my surprise, I was invited to participate in building a big beautiful skatepark, SkateStreet, in Ventura, California, and I joined forces with JW and his pals once again.

This is the story of how it all unfolded; how our ramp building evolved, how tribes of skaters welcomed us, and how hidden hands seemed to be helping us every step of the way.

Chapter 1 The Legend of Skateboarding

In the foggy back roads of time, my memories, all black and white and flickering, I was 10 years old in 1954. I grew up in Los Angeles County, first Long Beach and San Pedro on the South facing coast, then the San Fernando Valley just to the North of L.A. over the Hollywood Hills. At the time, there was no such thing as a skateboard. There was roller-skating. Unless you were committed enough to own shoe skates, typical roller skates clamped on to the bottom of your leather shoes, gripping the hard edge of the sole near the toes, with a strap around the ankle holding your shoe against the heel. A "skate-key" was the wrench that could make the adjustments in the length and width, so that they could fit a wide range of shoe sizes. The wheels were steel as well as everything else but the leather straps.

So as a kid in the 1940's and 50's, among the miscellaneous junk you had in your environment were these skates that had broken, worn out or had lost parts or had been left out in the rain. The adjustability of these clamp-on skates to accommodate all sizes was such that the heel portion and the toe portion could be expanded to about 10 inches and then they came apart. So it was natural and obvious with his innate engineering skills, that a kid would come to the conclusion that these heel and toe elements could be placed even farther apart, creating some kind of vehicle you could sit on or stand on.

Your typical creation was to nail the heel and toe wheels to a 2" x 4" about 3 feet long, then attach a wooden peach crate or fruit box, common in those days, upright on the nose end of the 2" x 4", nail a 1" x 2" on the top of the box, sticking out far enough to serve as handles, and there you had it; a scooter. These things were fun. They turned the sidewalks into racetracks. We'd made gizmos like this since I was 5 or 6 in San Pedro where there were sidewalks, but after 1950, we lived in the semi-rural San Fernando Valley.

There were no sidewalks in our neighborhood, but at a friend's house just up the street, there was a large smooth driveway and network of concrete walkways… a skatepark. We hammered together a couple of these peach box scooters, and had spent the afternoon hours careening about, piling up on the lawns, until it got dark. At ten years old, I got really wired by the experience. The one sleepwalking episode in my life was the night after one of those sessions. In our house in Northridge, in the middle of the night, my parents were jolted awake by the racket of me on this scooter, with its steel wheels on the hardwood floors as loud as a bowling alley. There I was, in some kind of a trance, riding back and forth in that hall, which was no more than twelve feet long. It was 3:00 in the morning. I know what an obsession that rolling, gliding sensation can be. They led me back to bed and I never woke up.

Kids all over LA, maybe all across the country, made similar scooters. Now the standard legend about skateboarding is that the peach box would break off, and it was discovered that it could still be ridden, hands free; thus, the original skateboard. My peach box never broke off, so somebody else had to invent "sidewalk surfing."

In 1958, we moved to Carpinteria, up the coast toward Santa Barbara, and I took up ocean surfing. I didn't get on an actual skateboard until about 1972.

Chapter 2 Hawaii The Perfect Wave

Right after JW was born in 1971, our commune moved into a big Victorian house in San Francisco. A couple of years later when we closed down that house, much of our tribe reconvened in different living arrangements on Hawaii's Big Island. People from that commune remain close friends to this day, and they'll keep cropping up in these stories. In 1975, JW's Mom, Patti, and I split up and I went back to the mainland to regroup in 1977.

In 1979, I was returning to Hawaii to settle down and enjoy the life of a single father. After a two-year absence on the mainland, I had some new skill sets.

I had worked one year each with two old friends from our extended Bay Area commune. I spent a year filling in the gaps in my understandings of house building with my old pal Gary Cohen. I spent the following year with another communal brother, Mark Taylor, building over sixty redwood hot tubs in the hills of Berkeley, Oakland and San Francisco, many with fancy environments of decks and fences. In June of that year, I was issued my California General Contractor's License, packed up four hot tubs and three Moonbeam side arm heaters and took my small bankroll to the Big Island.

By 1983, after a few bobbles, I had found a groove, and life was mellow. I was nearing my fortieth birthday, and had realized a dream of living a really basic lifestyle building simple houses on the tropical lava flows of East Hawaii. My son was 12, and we were living in one of three off-the-grid houses that the two of us had built on the edge of the rainforest. We had three dogs, nine when Hokulea had her puppies, two of which we kept. And at one time, we had at least seven surfboards.

When JW had expressed interest in surfing a few years earlier, we had gone down to Gaughen's Emporium, a friend's secondhand store at Keaau Junction, where the Pahoa Road meets Volcano Highway. We made a deal for every used surfboard in the place. I think there were about six, and the whole bill came to $95.00. I had revolving credit with my good friend Tim Gaughen. Funny things seemed happen in and around Gaughen's Emporium. I could pretty much take anything in the store and pay it off in carpentry later... always a good deal since Tim was a lot of fun to work with. There was always something to be done to upgrade and enhance the Emporium, and I was the guy. We peddled a small number of the hot tubs through there that I had brought with me from the mainland. I was Tim's go-to guy for lots of little projects around Puna. We nearly doubled the size of his rambling household in Volcano Village.

With Tim, we once built a house by buying odd lots of lumber of miscellaneous dimensions at this annual odd lot sale at the Hawaii Planing Mill, trucked it out to a cloud forest clearing in Volcano, and just built what came to mind given the situation, the space, the lumber pile and the collective imaginations of those present on any given day. Then, after it was completed, I drafted the plans for it; then, I got the permit for it; then, next day, they sent an inspector out. It was a dreamtime for me, bringing house building to the art form that it can be when the permit process is out of the way. Building what you want in the moment, then getting permission later is a rare thing these days. But it was laid back Hawaii, and in that time and place I was well enough known in the building department that the bureaucratic details could be satisfied at the last stroke, not the first.

Anyway, we took all these surfboards home, lined them all up in JW's room. Some we picked out for him to try in the water, some needed repair first, some we just chopped up for parts or stripped for our reshaping experiments. We made a belly board out of one. How it feels to shape the foam, lay the fiberglass and to know that smell of acetone, acrylic resins and epoxy become nostalgic sensations to a surfer. They are nasty toxic chemicals you wouldn't want to spend a lot of time in a closed space with, so we used them outside.

A few miles North of Hilo on the East-facing coast of the Big Island, Honoli'i Stream meets the ocean below high red bluffs. In one legend, it's the place where the demi-god Maui met his end. The river-mouth and bottom conditions make an excellent surf spot with multiple zones for different levels of skill: a dependable, often overhead and occasionally tubular left north of the river-mouth channel, medium sized lefts and rights mid-channel, and an easy small shorebreak over shallow water near the beach. Waiting on the outside between sets, the Honu sea turtles bob up so close to you that you catch a whiff of their wet garbage bad breath, before they return to foraging on the bottom.

JW was always a high-energy action figure kind of a kid, and easily took to surfing. Over repeated trips to Honoli'i he taught himself the basics, and tested our different surfboards. Before long he knew which one to ride, and how to fix the dings from his crackups, repairs of either fiberglass or flesh; how to install a fin block or leash plug; and he discovered the moving terrain and kinetics of the ocean that you can only learn through getting out there and playing in it.

Well, turn the pages on this scene a few years and we've got this: We're up early on a Sunday morning, got our papaya right off the tree, we've gone down to Pahoa to get the Sunday Hilo Tribune, eggs and rice; coffee for me and guava nectar for JW at the Circle J; then continued on down a road that was lined on both sides with mango trees, through a mango tunnel, along a mango road slippery with fallen mangoes, through a gauntlet of falling mangoes, denting the truck, to a place along a jagged lava coast near Pohoiki Bay known locally as "Shacks."

JW reads the funnies and then hits the water while I spend a little more time with the news and coffee.

Finally, about 8:00, I get out of the truck, wax up the surfboard, strap on the leash, and walk into the water. There are hot volcanic springs along this part of the coast, and right where we go into the water, the temperature is just about like getting into a bathtub; the water gets cooler as you paddle out. It's an easy paddle to a big square-edged underwater shelf, where the molten lava cooled abruptly to a stop. There, the deep ocean swells jump up as square-top head-high made-for-surfing wavewalls that peel off evenly. After an hour in a watery no-mind of gliding in the waves and sunlight, in these ideal conditions, JW and I are sitting on our boards, bobbing in silence in a glassy calm between sets ...and we look around, and realize that we are the only people there ...9:00 AM on Sunday in heaven. Heaven is a momentary state of mind, available to all who look for it; but in surfing, there are some days that line up better than others.

It's not always a clear sunny day in Hawaii with head-high walls all to yourself, but along with the invention and evolution of the skateboard, there comes a generation that learns to "surf" the streets, parking lots, parks, drainage ditches, empty swimming pools, chunks of broken concrete, and warehouses and all manner of inanimate objects: and thus, surf can be found in any weather and the "surf'" is up whenever a skater's energy and imagination are up. Better still for me; <u>the perfect wave can be built,</u> in plywood and Masonite; and the possible configurations of ideal terrain and riding surfaces are endless. That's where I came in; I got to build some really cool stuff skaters thought of.

We lived way beyond the end of the power and phone lines, water and sewer and gas lines, way out in the sticks of East Hawaii beyond the paved roads. Our road was a bulldozer track along the edge of the rainforest surfaced with red volcanic cinder; you could run on it, you could ride a bike on it, but you couldn't skateboard on it.

JW's Mom, Patti, lived down by Hilo Bay on the north-facing coast and often on the weekends he would go down to stay at her house. She had a good surf spot nearby at Four Mile, and she had a little pavement, a driveway. When the surf was flat, JW would take to tapping up and down on his skateboard in her driveway and before long he wanted to have some kind of banked obstacle that he could set up to practice kick turns on.

Skaters learn the fundamentals of structure by leaning a piece of plywood against something and trying to skate on it, or off it, or up it, or over it. The thing slides, or it falls, or it sags or it bends, or it breaks ...or it works! Ramp building is figuring out how to prop things up better.

JW had a piece of 5/8" plywood that was half of a circular cutout from the skylight at our Ainaloa house, and we beefed it up with 2" x 4"s and a hinged leg so he could put it away in his mom's garage and not take up too much space. At that initial level of skateboarding, you just need a little banked surface to develop the basic skill of the kickturn right in your own driveway.

When I had returned to the Big Island in 1979, it was agreed that JW would come to live with me out in Pahoa, in the Puna district. I arrived that summer and immediately found projects in the heart of town. JW was going to come live with me when school started in September. Pahoa Elementary had the outward appearance of a upstanding school but during the summer I had heard increasingly alarming stories about what went on there; the belligerence and violence, the racial divisions among the kids. I learned that just that spring, some seventh grade girls had lured a fifth grade boy into the girl's bathroom and stabbed him over some marijuana taken from someone's locker, and he died. I began to think that my Puna plan was not such a good idea after all. The team slogan at Pahoa Elementary was, "Home of the Daggers." Sheesh...But by that time, I was committed; I had spent most of my resources buying a fixer upper off the grid in nearby Ainaloa, and that's where we were going to live.

Then I got the word about Malamalama School, a hippy school in Opihikao, above the Southeast facing Kalapana coast. About three acres of a sugarcane field had been cleared and a mowed grass lawn was maintained. It was the homestead of David and Donna Gradwohl and their three kids, the oldest of which was JW's age. They were determined to provide a quality school experience for them and had rounded up enough like-minded parents and resources to pull it off. Two simple schoolhouses had been built and three grade levels were being conducted. Here, the teacher for JW's class, Mr. Greenlaw, led the class in singing "We All Live in a Yellow Submarine" each morning. Much better.

Among the parents there were Klip and Kathy. Kathy had two boys, Brian and Henry, one in JW's class. Without the four of them, JW's attending Malamalama School would not have been possible. They provided a place to hang out after school and a ride to and from. Occasionally, they hired me to build stuff on their property in Leilani. Like many homesteads in Puna, the roads and driveways were bulldozed tracks through the jungle, surfaced with red volcanic cinders. Their yard and buildings sat in a clearing surrounded by huge Hapu'u ferns and Ohi'a trees. The compound consisted of the original round yurt-like building dominated by a kitchen, and a two-story house built at a later time with three bedrooms upstairs, and the entire downstairs was devoted to making music. There was a piano, a drum set, clarinet, violin, miscellaneous guitars, amps and a saxophone. Klip played the sax with a jazz group at the local tavern in Pahoa, and would often have his buddies over to the house to jam.

The first thing they asked me to work on was a huge crudely built roof that covered the outdoor space between the two buildings. The building inspector had some problem with it. I took a quick look and thereafter refused to go underneath; I wouldn't even go under to talk about it out of the rain. Klip said the building inspector had acted the same way. There wasn't a lot holding it up. So my first project was to build a big roof structure, with properly sized beams, post and braces. Over the years, I was called upon to make lots of smaller improvements.

One day Klip decided that he wanted a skateboard ramp, a small halfpipe for the kids. They didn't have any skateable surfaces at their place either. I was naturally the guy to do it. I bought the latest skateboard magazines figuring there would be an ad for ramp plans. I never found such an ad but I learned enough, I thought, by looking at the pictures. What did catch my eye, though, was something that's a shock to any parent; an article entitled something to the effect of "How To Regain Your Nerve After Your First Major Injury." Oh great. It assumed that there would be major injury... and more than one. So I turned to J.W. and asked if he wouldn't like it just as well if he stuck to some sport where there's something soft to land on like water ...or snow. He reminds me of the two occasions he witnessed me bloodying my back bouncing off the reef at Pohoiki Bay, and another time, coming out of the water with a deep coral gash in my foot at Kalapana, and all the stories of catastrophe and mayhem in the surf when I was younger. "OK, OK," I said, "adventure's not safe ...of course it's not safe." Theme parks are safe. Watching TV is safe: Life's real adventures are not safe. Learn first aid, and go ahead on.

The trouble with the Leilani ramp was that it became obsolete before it was even finished ...before we were skinning it with Masonite, the kids were riding and realizing that they were going to want it wider, and higher: and I was realizing that it wasn't built so that it could be easily expanded. It was fun, but flawed in that way. It was an important lesson in rampbuilding: Build with the expectation of evolution. In this case, I cantilevered the joists of the skating surface over the edge of the bulkheads. This made the ramp more difficult to add to, to widen. These creations are going to be remodeled and recycled endlessly. The skaters will always want it wider and higher: more, more. There will be need to move the ramp, for a variety of reasons. So the common structure of ramps is modular, so that the cannibalized parts can be part of future incarnations. Still, the Leilani ramp was big fun and served the purpose of advancing the kids' skills; mine too. I never found the article about how to build a skateboard ramp, but now that I've written this book, folks aren't going to have that problem.

During our six years in Puna, Malamalama School had morphed into a Waldorf School with a nice big new building in Paradise Park, closer to where we lived in Ainaloa. The school had kept adding a new grade each year, keeping up with that original age group in Mr. Greenlaw's yellow submarine. By 1985, JW's class was high school age, and Malamalama School could no longer keep up with expanding needs for facilities and teachers. JW spent one year at Hilo High, staying with his Mom during the week. I figured it was time to move to the mainland.

Chapter 3 Anti Gravity Device Company

When you need a job, congratulations, you've made it to square one of a new adventure.

We arrived in California in 1986 and located ourselves in the little beach town of Carpinteria, my hometown, just a few minutes down the coast from Santa Barbara. JW enrolled in the local high school, where I had graduated in 1961, and my Mom, too, in 1930. I needed a job fast. Since I didn't know anybody in Santa Barbara, I would have to start from scratch. I was following up any newspaper ad that I remotely qualified for, but not much was popping up in the way of construction. Then there appeared an ad for a screen-printer, right in Carpinteria. ...Hmmm, I can do that.

JW and I had done some simple silkscreen printing in Hawaii, where we carried our photo emulsion-coated screens outside in the noonday tropical sun and removed the tarpaper cover for a timed interval to expose them. J.W. had various dragon motif screens, and I made some shirts for Gaughen's Emporium and when we were leaving, a "Tankers Can Fly" depicting a transcendent longboard surfer leaving Earth, from the Big Island, in the distant background.

The screen-printing plant was about a block and a

half from my grandparents' house where my family had lived off and on from 1944 up through High School in 1961. The company's name was Shirts, Inc. and it was housed in one of the old lemon-packing houses next to the railroad tracks that we used to crawl under as part of our childhood "short cut" to the beach. It wasn't shorter but since it was forbidden, it was preferred. They had a proper darkroom for burning screens, a battery of hand printing stations and a big rotary autopress. I picked it up really quickly and by the end of the 9 months that I worked there, they were offering to make me a production manager, and run a night shift.

JW was the new kid in town and in the evenings after he convinced me that homework was done, he'd go out on the streets with his skateboard to make friends and work on his skating skills. After a while, he had a group of buddies that liked to surf and skate together: Alfredo, Christian, Nashia, Judd and Jesse. I stayed involved by providing the transportation for their expeditions. There were some decent surf spots right in town; Tar Pits and Jellybowl, but there was occasionally world class surf at Rincon Point about three miles down the coast and a reliable shorebreak at La Conchita, a couple miles more, and a point we used to call Knickerbockers a mile more.

Shirts, Inc. participated in the bi-annual Action Sports Retailers trade show, usually held in Long Beach, California, city of my birth. The company had a small exhibit there. When I realized what it was, I arranged for JW and I to be included. It was the venue where all manufacturers of boogie boards, surfboards, sneakers, snowboards, sunglasses, suntan lotion, skateboards, swimwear came to display their wares for the retailers that would be stocking and selling them, By the time the second ASR show came around, I had come up with a strategy that would get JW and I in every time. All you had to do was come up with a trade name, subscribe to their magazine, Action Sports Retailer, and you were in. So I came up with a name, "Anti Gravity Device Company" (code for skateboard ramps), checked the box "manufacturer," listed myself and JW as president and vice president, paid the $35 for a yearly subscription, and we were in. Obviously, there was a world of livelihoods in the creating, manufacturing, selling, promoting the products and lifestyle of action sports; California, youth culture, the beach, the snow, the surf; and now, the asphalt and concrete, plywood and Masonite. I was looking for a way to get us in the game.

The surf around Carpinteria is sporadic. The Channel Islands, 20-30 miles offshore protects our coast from most south swells, and Point Conception where the coast turns from east-west to north-south, juts out just enough to shield the whole Santa Barbara oceanfront from the predominant swell from the northwest. It's the rare West swell that fills the channel with energy and brings out the best of our coastline. JW grew up surfing the warm, clear water and abundant swells of Hawaii that California could never match. There wasn't enough surf to keep JW occupied, so to stay involved myself, I would take JW and his pals from Carpinteria on little excursions around the area looking for both surfable surf and skateable terrain: Walls, ditches, downhills, backyard ramps.

Flashback: I spent my high school years and a few years after that in Carpinteria. Besides having beautiful beaches, the fun shore breaks, and Rincon so close that you could hit the surf before school, Carp had another amazing resource; the beach camp. During the summer months, the camp was loaded with families camping, most of them from Los Angeles or Orange Counties. With them, of course, were their teenage daughters, away from their usual boyfriends, hoping to have some fun, and primed for short-term summer romance. My Mom, who had graduated from high school here in 1930, reported the same phenomenon when she was young. Young people of her age, boys and girls, characteristically put their school year relationships on hold for the summer months to take advantage of the situation, and paired up again in September.

There was a rectangular cruising circuit from Highway 101 down the main drag, Linden avenue, to the Main Beach, then left to the Beach Camp, left up Palm Avenue back up to 101, now known as Carpinteria Avenue, left to Linden, and back down to the beach...or the other way around. Invariably, girls would be walking to town in pairs, looking for something to do. Now there was one factor that might have seemed not quite so perfect on the surface. In the early summer, up through July, it was about a fifty-fifty chance that the whole town was enveloped in a cool fog on any given day. To the vacationing campers from L.A., fog was a bummer. To some of us beach town cruisers, this was good news as much as a sunny day if you shifted gears. The girls would be bored, and extra ready to hop in a car with some local boys with a fun idea. There were lots of things to do that just required a car and some local knowledge.

Montecito is about 7 miles up the coast from Carp. It is where the rich and famous had, and still have, fabulous estates. Up one of the back roads, there was an abandoned estate we called The Tea Gardens. There were large iron gates attached to substantial stone pillars, a smaller gate, and a small stone building, possibly a sentry post, next to the entrance. The gates were always chained shut, but it was no problem to find a way in. There was over, under or around. Once in, the road wound uphill, through a dry oak, manzanita and toyon forest left wild, through an amazing set of features. The property had been developed as a hedonist's pleasure park. An enormous concrete waterworks, starting with two reservoirs at the top, fed through concrete channels down to large swimming pools. These were no ordinary swimming pools. They were huge, and lined with platforms for lying about, Greek-looking columns and at one time statues, though my memory is hazy about whether the statues remained in 1961. All of the pools and reservoirs were bone dry, due to cracks in the concrete and decades of neglect. The plot was, however, to entertain and enjoy our new friends in this truly exotic environment in the dusk and early evening with wonder of the surroundings and ghost stories, and have them back at the beach camp by 11:00 or so. That's the "foggy day principle," that a silver lining may be found in life's apparent gloom. That might be another of my good luck charms, watch for it: "Foggy day? What amazing good fortune!"

Back to the point: To my surprise, twenty-five years later, the estate was still abandoned, and these empty pools and reservoirs had become an accidental skatepark of crumbling waterworks. The largest reservoir had been dubbed "Tea bowl," and higher up at the very top of the hill, a dry shallow reservoir with the lumpy bottom was appropriately named "Moguls." All decorated with skaters' graffiti art.

There are several ways to categorize skate-boarding. It can be broken down into Freestyle Skating, Street Skating, and Vert Skating. At least those were the categories of skate contests.

Freestyle skating is done in a small area of flat ground and consists of techniques of gymnastics and board manipulation with the hands and feet. It is the purist form of skating in a way. It is the laboratory of what can be done with a human body and a skate-board. It is focused, intellectual and technical. It serves as a proving ground for what can be done while in the ballistic motion in the street, and what can be done while in the weightless state of vert.

What is termed street skating should be considered the highest form of the art, in the sense that the terrain is the least contrived. The skating surfaces are "found art;" the accidental topography of sidewalks, curbs, pavement, swales, banks, drainage ditches, flood channels, reservoirs, dams, tunnels, stairs, railings, planters; in short what we in construction call "hardscape." In the mind of a skater, all this urban hardscape becomes an elaborate ski slope; a free form rollercoaster, a concrete and asphalt amusement park, and all the rides are free. Your ticket to ride is this simple device: a skateboard, trucks and wheels and your own skill and courage in riding it.

Street skaters don't need the world to be created for them; they create it out of what is there, in the moment. That's what they had at the Tea Gardens. Heaven doesn't need to be built. Heaven can be found. It is spread upon the earth and pedestrians do not see it.

Vert skating is the most dramatic form of skating and most akin to flying. Vert skating was the outgrowth of skating empty swimming pools during an extended California drought (foggy day principle...No water for your pool? What amazing good fortune!) Having a skating surface that curved up smoothly to a vertical plane began to create possibilities of an extended weightless state; flying. Recreating the geometry of swimming pools out of plywood were the earl halfpipes." It was discovered that the addition of an expanse of "flatbottom" allowed the skater to have two opportunities to finesse his momentum by pumping twice: once the transition from vertical to horizontal, across the flatbottom, once on the transition from horizontal back to vertical. More speed makes more weightless time, higher flying. They are called halfpipes, but they would be more accurately be described as two quarter pipes connected by a flatbottom. That's your basic halfpipe dimensions: radius of transitions, the height that the transitions are cut off, or if they go all the way to vertical, then the amount of vertical, by however wide you want. If the transition is cut off before it reaches vertical it's called a mini ramp. If the ramp goes all the way plus some vertical, it's called a vert ramp. So there you go:

HALFPIPE + SKATEBOARD = ANTI GRAVITY DEVICE

Then there's the idea of skatepark skating; where every form of skating can be created, combined, idealized and maximized in one location. When I was younger and imagining how my building career might proceed, I had a dream to build an actual wood timber roller coaster, like the Cyclone Racer at the Long Beach Pike, or the Sea Serpent at Pacific Ocean Park in Santa Monica that I enjoyed as a kid. Over the years my dream morphed into the desire to build a skateboard park.

What a roller coaster does is to provide safe thrills for couch potatoes, strapped into a rolling couch sent through a rigidly defined loop. A skatepark is a roller coaster for the skilled and the brave, careening through a unique path in the moment.

Chapter 4 Finding Animal Chin

Well, then this fateful thing began to unfold for us. This time, JW needed a job, and what he found was the portal to our big new adventure. He went to work at the local surf and skate store there in Carpinteria called the "Sunshine Store." One day, in the spring of 1987, his boss Bernie gave him two complimentary tickets to the "Premiere" of a new skateboard video produced by a big skateboard manufacturer based in Santa Barbara, Powell-Peralta. Being a great son, he wanted to keep me involved, so he offered me the other ticket.

Down the rabbit hole we went.

The Santa Barbara premiere was held in the old Mission Theater on lower State Street that has since been torn down. It wasn't an event you could buy a ticket for. All these kids had some connection to the people who made their living through, or had some committed involvement in the Santa Barbara skateboard world. The line went down the block; there were mostly excited young skaters like JW, and a few older skaters, and skateshop owners. When we entered, each person was handed a soda and a box of popcorn and as we turned to go to our seats, there in the middle of this swarming lobby was a white haired and bearded gentlemen who I immediately recognized as a nearly mythical figure out of my past, looking exactly as he did when I had seen him last, decades before. His name was Vernon Johnson...In the 1950's he created quite a stir by purchasing an old Santa Barbara Transit Co. bus, loading his whole family, his wife and eight kids in it, and going for a tour across Russia!

This man may have saved us all from nuclear annihilation. In September of 1959, Nikita Khrushchev, premier of the Soviet Union, was visiting the United States. The premier had in his power the ability to set off World War III, a worldwide conflagration.

I lived in Carpinteria the last three years of high school. Khrushchev would be passing through town on a train. The press was reporting that he was miffed by not being allowed to visit Disneyland due to security concerns, and generally having a rotten time in Los Angeles, with crowds of protestors throwing tomatoes at his limousine and in the dust-up about that in the days that followed, a grumpy Khrushchev was taking his planned high security train trip up our scenic coast. He was having a very bad time.

Escorted by helicopters, a two-train caravan rumbled on through town and on toward Santa Barbara. It was strange. This was the man who had proclaimed to the West, "We will bury you," a year before. At school, fire drills routinely alternated with nuclear attack drills. This was the man whose bombs we practiced ducking under our desks to shield ourselves from. Two years earlier, the USSR had launched their Sputnik satellite, the first man-made object in earth orbit. The American space efforts were definitely behind, and it was proof that our foremost Cold War adversary could deliver a nuclear bomb to anyplace in the world. This was the man who could make the order. He was riding through town on a sunny September Sunday, and it didn't seem fearful. I watched him go by down where the little railroad bridge at the slough crosses Carpinteria Creek near the ocean. I was lying on the ice-plant-covered sand dune at the beach camp, and there he goes: the great bogeyman.

In Santa Barbara, it was wondered if he would be in a good enough mood to even get off the train to greet local dignitaries. When the train stopped it was reported that he sat there glowering until he had became aware of a smiling bearded face in the crowd. Only then did he decide to get off the train. He got out, and after a perfunctory shaking of hands with the mayor; he oddly singled out the man in the crowd who looked interesting to him, the man with a short white beard. They had a brief exchange through an interpreter in which the bearded one welcomed him to Santa Barbara and expressed an interest in visiting Russia. And the chairman of the Union of Soviet Socialists Republic said, to the effect, "Come on over."

Khrushchev's mood was decidedly elevated by this short conversation, and World War III never happened.

The following year this man, Vernon Johnson, with his wife and eight kids, left California on a personal good will mission, driving across the U.S, then a ship to Italy, then driving up through Europe and on to a momentary encounter with Khrushchev in Moscow. During the Cuban Missile Crisis, just two years later, his finger hovered over the doomsday button. How could he incinerate the Johnsons?

It was a very bizarre but far-sighted thing to be doing at the height of the Cold War, to be cutting through the crap like that. In the public schools there were entire programs of political paranoia coaching us as to how to spot propaganda being directed at us (we learned, all right); with fire drills we marched outside and lined up on the playground; with nuclear blast drills we dove under our desks "keep your backs to the windows, there will be flying glass and an eyeball destroying blinding flash." So in the midst of the hype of this Russian-atheist-Communist-menace, one guy turns to his wife and says, "Why don't we load all the kids in a bus and go half way around the world and see for ourselves?" And she says, "OK", and off they go.

Well, after a while they come back alive and were a feature in the local newspaper for a time, but then I didn't hear about them for a few years. I'm not sure when, but they next came on my radar when they were central in building a village of small non-code structures in the area of Hollister Ranch where they were experimenting with different communal arrangements, another ahead-of-the-times thing to be doing in the early sixties, until the Sheriff's Department, Health Department and Building Department showed up to close them down. They were non-conformists, like beatniks, only optimistic. They were hippies before the word had been coined. Bohemians you might say, free thinkers. Life as an experimental adventure.

A few years later, I was 18 in 1962 and alternating between college and surfing escapades and work. I had landed a job as a gopher for a real estate broker in Santa Barbara–collecting rents, placing ads, setting up For Sale signs, plowing the weeds under on a vacant lot–stuff like that. I was doing that for only a couple months when the broker tells me he's not going to do real estate anymore, because a friend of his is running for Congress and he's going to put everything into that ...and this friend is: Vern Johnson.

So for the next few months, I was paid the same rate to be a campaign gopher for this local legend. To make a long story short, I had a grand adventure, got my young brain spun around in many curious and unexpected ways, and when VJ lost the election, I went back to UCSB and eventually changed my focus to Political Science and Eastern philosophy. Most of all, the lesson was that life could be, should be, built around the pursuit of happiness, beyond the boundaries of what has come before, and love for however big a family as you can conceive yourself being a part of.

Then, quarter of a century later, I returned to Santa

Barbara with my own teenage son and there in the middle of a crowd of excited skateboarders stands Vern Johnson, beaming with bliss at the whole spectacle ...with white hair and short white beard, he looks exactly as he did the last time I saw him about twenty-five years before. I go up and shake his hand and explain how it is that I recognize him and we have a few laughs as the mob swarms past us. I find out why he's here. He says that he's "part of the family" in this skateboard company. The fact that he's there gives me a feeling this night is fateful, as it has turned out to be. He was always ahead of his time and at this moment he's the symbolic patriarch of this skateboard scene. As I learned later, it turns out that three of those kids he took with him across Russia were part of that skateboard company. One daughter, Christie, was married to the company president, George Powell; another daughter, Jill, was the company's buyer, and his son, Court Johnson, VCJ, was the company's artist, creator of most of the logos adorning the skateboards, wheels, stickers and t-shirts.

The theater was packed with excited young skaters; a large video projector was propped on some seats in the middle, ready to go. Someone named Stacy Peralta was introduced and cheers went up in the crowd. He was the director of the movie, and known pretty much as one the first skateboarders to actually make a career of it. He was a hero to all these kids. He had invented being a skateboard pro. He was "older" now, in his late twenties, and had gathered a team of younger skaters, "The Bones Brigade."

Well, the video was called, The Search For Animal Chin...and the thin plot is that a group of skaters are trying to catch up with an elusive sort of Zen master of skateboarding. The supposed search for him in various parts of California, Nevada and Hawaii was an excuse to show off these five professional skaters in some great skate spots...They never do catch up with Animal Chin, but the point of the allegory is a journey in search of fun...search for the sweet spots...pursuit of happiness...which is what skateboarding is all about, and for me, what ramp building was all about.

The five skaters featured in this video, besides being astounding athletes, are fine human beings as well, and having eventually met each of them briefly, and followed their careers over the years, I know each of them to be a class act. This was a remarkable collection of photogenic and charismatic good people.

The movie begins with a grinning skeleton, ripping through the black screen, exposing his skull, posing like the MGM lion, and then laughing hoarsely in the place of the lion's roar. From the very beginning, the film mocks every part of the pop culture it portrays, including mocking itself. This movie is a funny, corny, hokie, high camp masterpiece. It's a feature length put-on. The acting ranges from reluctant, to amateurish and occasionally inspired, simply because the characters are not actors, they are playing themselves. The special effects are intentionally transparent and low tech. The soundtrack music was original and exceptional. If the goal was to present skating in its most accessible form, they nailed it. The five members of the "Bones Brigade" were a mismatched collection of skaters, exactly the same kind of mixture that JW and every young skater was experiencing with his own local mismatched brigade of buddies from his own neighborhood.

The production had the feel of a movie created by the teenage skaters that it featured. Its genius is cloaked in silliness. Genius might not be the word for it, since years later I learned that Stacy was surprised to see Animal Chin become such big success and an influence on so many people. As a professional, its flaws were glaring to him, but invisible to the rest of us. So some of the movie's genius was accidental, but unmistakable is the truth in its portrayal of the joy of skating, and of being a skater, and it totally worked for JW and me.

There is nothing in the plot line that involves worldly pedestrian motives. Not sex, not drugs, not money, romance, greed or power, not even good or evil. It's propelled by the rolling pursuit of fun. If it were a surf movie, the settings would be distant and exotic surf spots out of reach of your average American kid. In the world of Animal Chin, all the destinations: the ditches, sidewalks, backyard ramps, and empty swimming pools are part of a skater's everyday environment. Even as much as the film is a preadolescent fantasy, it has the edginess that the skating itself is real, and beyond acting. The skating is absolutely genuine, impossible to fake, and physically dangerous and obviously really, really fun. And ordinary kids were the world champions of it. All they needed was this simple set up–a skateboard, trucks, bearings and wheels. The world champs rode the same equipment that any kid could buy in his local skateshop–the exact same equipment. Powell-Peralta products, top quality, ran about $150.

Well, anyway, in the theater there I'm enjoying myself having some easy laughs and marveling at the skills of the "Bones Brigade." I'm getting a better idea of what a skater can do, and charmed by the similarities of a skate safari to the surf trips I used to take up and down this coast. Toward the end of the video the skaters arrive at "The Chin Ramp." When I see this thing I'm amazed and startled, and I'm hit with the sinking feeling in my gut that I had missed out on being in on the building of something never to be repeated...an "I got-here-just-a-little-too-late" sort of feeling. It was huge, and had been built solely for the video and was torn down a few weeks after filming.

When we left the theater that night, I came away with three revelations. First, the Bones Brigade riders had showcased skating way beyond what I could have imagined physically; their skills were mind-boggling. Second, with this new idea of what was possible, I had more of a street skater's eye, and as I went about my everyday travels, I was able to see the possibilities presented by this asphalt and concrete surf that's everywhere. So, when driving for JW and his pals, exploring the back roads and alleys of Southern

California I had a new perspective, I knew what to look for. The third idea was that I really, really wanted to participate in the building of something on the level of that Chin Ramp.

We didn't have a VCR at the time, but I bought a copy of the video before we left the theater anyway. It was early May, and when JW and I went back to Hawaii that summer a month later, we took that copy of Animal Chin with us, showed it all around to our pals. We must have watched it 15 times. To us, it was a life-changing work of art. JW got to drawing pictures of the Chin Ramp and we worked out the dimensions as best we could from freeze-framing the tape and counting the seams in the 4' x 8' sheets of plywood.

When we got back from Hawaii at the end of that summer, I needed a job. Powell Corporation had put a classified ad in the Santa Barbara News-Press for a "facilities carpenter." I think I was the first one to answer the ad. It was like going to a movie, and then going to live inside the movie.

Chapter 5 Powell-Peralta 1987

The Powell-Peralta offices, warehouse, art department and manufacturing were housed in about five or six small nondescript commercial buildings on Gutierrez Street in lower East Side Santa Barbara, with no signs to identify them. The company had started out in a garage somewhere, moved to a little larger place, added another, and another, right around in the same neighborhood.

I showed up that Monday morning and was met by Joel Watson. It wasn't clear what Joel's title was, and he liked it that way. There wasn't much of an organizational chart at Powell, and he liked it that way. The old personnel manager had left and the new one was due to start the following week, so for the moment there wasn't any personnel manager at all, and Joel liked that especially. He could hire on his sole say-so. You kind of got the feeling that Joel didn't have much tolerance for corporate B.S., and that would get him in trouble from time to time, and he even liked that, too.

Joel was the kind that would throw the résumé in the trash and look you in the eye and ask a few direct questions, then go with his hunch ...which was good for me, since my résumé listed 10 people I had built houses for in distant Hawaii, and my only mainland references were the 9 months I had spent at Shirts,

Inc., and my California Contractor's license from 1979.

Anyway, I got the job. I remember the day I told JW that I had landed a job with the legendary Powell-Peralta. I hadn't told him about the interview ahead of time, not wanting to get his hopes up. We were deliriously ecstatic about our unbelievable good fortune. And I must say, over the decades since, we made the most of it.

When I started working there, the company was having an exceptional 30 million dollar year, and was selling everything it could produce, trying to catch up with back orders and expanding production, renting additional space. Facilities didn't have a shop, and the company didn't have a skateboard ramp they could call their own and fortunately, they didn't have somebody with my particular set of skills.

They did have a riverboat mechanic from Missouri, who was our leader, Joel. Next, a grizzly-looking biker, our shop foreman Peter Edwards; and a hippy surfer funnyman, painter, fiberglasser, airbrush artist and general cut-up, Ves Fowler; and a barefoot mountain boy, James Gardner, was the electronics guy and computer tech. That was the Facilities crew when I got there.

Joel was in charge of Facilities and whatever else he could stick his nose into and there were plenty of peripheral projects that Facilities was involved in that were beyond the realm of an ordinary factory maintenance crew. There were the twice-a-year ASR trade shows in Long Beach that were attended by thousands of "action sports retailers" and Facilities would produce whatever the design group thought up...and they got pretty elaborate.

Peter Edwards was my original foreman. Peter, you might say, was very fashion conscious. He invariably wore the same style. He never cut his hair or beard, wore a dark baseball cap, Levi's, wallet in the back pocket on a chain, motorcycle boots, and under his jacket, a black t-shirt always with a Harley Davidson logo, usually from one of their innumerable local dealers around Southern California. His pride and joy, of course, was a beautiful classic Harley: a "Pan-head." His skills included a broad range of mechanical and metalworking skills and big rig truck driving. Like most of my friends, he was really good at what he did.

The position required him to supervise the construction of our trade show exhibits, with the object of knocking them down, packing the parts into large reinforced reusable shipping crates that could be fork lifted onto a flat bed truck or trailer, and strong enough to be left to the union workers who would unload them at the convention center. It was the same trade show that JW and I had been attending as execs of Anti Gravity Device Company.

Facilities didn't have a shop at first. We could set up a shop and a table saw in the warehouse loading dock, but we had to knock it down at a moment's notice when the UPS truck came. I first encountered Chris

Iverson when he came skating off that loading dock with a clipboard in his hand, taking the four-foot drop nonchalantly, hardly looking up from his reading. In a few months Facilities began to share some shop space with Chris and his R&D department behind a couple of roll up doors in an alley around the corner from the company offices. R&D's function was to test the company's various products. I got to know Chris who over time became a very close friend. Chris was the key to joining forces in ramp building, since those efforts were ordinarily not done on company time, but by volunteers among the employees who were skaters, and me...and before long, JW.

Events were moving fast when I came on board. The scene in Santa Barbara was the manufacturing end of the business. The team riders, "The Bones Brigade," had come from all over, but by that time they all lived on the West coast. Stacy Peralta and his video making crews, as well as Lance Mountain and Rodney Mullen were in the Los Angeles area, Tony Hawk and Mike McGill lived farther south toward San Diego, Tommy Guerrero and Steve Caballero were from the San Francisco Bay Area of Northern California, and Kevin Harris was from Vancouver.

The company would occasionally gather them all together for a photo shoot for different ads and promotional purposes, and to make it all worth their while and have it be a fun thing for them to come to Santa Barbara, the company created a skate session. One of the first things I did at Powell was to get ready for one of those events. The company had rented some warehouse space in the "Ver-Cal" building, about 10 blocks from the main cluster of buildings in lower East Side SB.

Chris had gotten hold of a mini-ramp in about six sections and Facilities had the job of putting it together for the one-night jam. We created a continuous 100-foot pair of heavy duty PVC pipes on a short stack of bolted-together 2" x 6"s so that the event could boast "world record rail slide," as if anybody cared about that. There was a launch ramp and a "fun box," a term for a skate element that starts out as a reinforced box with any number of launch ramp and rail slide attachments. When I realized that the amateur team was going to be there as well as the pros; and that skaters who worked at the company were also welcome, that was JW's opening. Joel said ask Todd Hastings, the team manger, and JW was in. The event, sort of the ultimate backstage of the skateboard world, was a party to skate with our team riders.

JW got there early and was helping bolt the last section of the rail slide together when the pros started skating in through the open door and charging the rail slide. In minutes, the team had mastered the 100-foot and could have gone even longer, sliding off the end with momentum to spare. As the evening went on, more and more skaters; pros, amateurs, and employees filled up the room. This was our first rudimentary skatepark: a mini-ramp and some street obstacles. JW was up on the crowded rollout of the halfpipe, waiting for his opportunity to drop in, when he realized that the legendary Tony Hawk was standing right next to him, waiting to drop in also. Tony turned to him and said, “After you!”

Chapter 6 Horton Building 1988

The company's hyphenated name, Powell-Peralta, had a good sound to it. Stacy Peralta was the video producer, creator of the Bones Brigade team and former professional skater. He lived in Los Angeles and we rarely saw him. George Powell was the CEO, the manufacturer, and on the job in Santa Barbara every day. George was a Stanford-trained aerospace engineer, who skateboarded the campus in his college days back when skateboard wheels were made of clay. One day, years later, when his own teenage son, Abe, came home with the news that someone came up with the simple idea of making urethane wheels for skateboards, the light bulb over George's head clicked on. That was right up his alley. Thereafter he put all his engineering skills into making innovative and quality equipment for skateboarding.

About the time the Ver-Cal event took place, Facilities got a building of its own, around the corner from R&D. It was referred to as the Horton Building. Peter had an office in the front corner and the 2000 square foot big room had roll-up doors in the front and back, and another approximately 3000 square foot storage yard in back. Out in front, an unmarked space was reserved for George Powell's car. George was always friendly and approachable, quiet and restrained, understated, a bit hard to read, and over the few years

I was there I came to think of him in terms that car. It was a Mercedes-Benz sedan, obviously his choice for the quality of engineering, and it was silver-gray, the most invisible finish available: a gray sedan. The mismatched collection of buildings that comprised the Powell offices, warehouses and production facilities were never painted or adorned with signage. Their exteriors all remained as we found them and there was no outward indication that the buildings were somehow a single manufacturing operation. That fact was invisible. Inside the focus of our actions was on the products. A year later when he purchased the big facility near the Santa Barbara Airport, he had the building completely renovated and upgraded in every way, remodeled to suit the needs of all our departments. And what color do you suppose he painted it? Gray. Actually, he went whole hog, ten shades of gray. Literally, I'm not kidding, ten different mixtures of black and white.

Imagine that underneath the bright colors of the graphics and wheels is the silver-gray Powell product of evolved engineering; and a big gray factory invisibly pumping out the top quality Powell-Peralta skateboard and wheels, the Mercedes-Benz of skateboarding. That's George's contribution, the unmatched quality of his invisible engineering.

Stacy Peralta never had to feel like he was fronting for products that were anything other than the best equipment in the industry. Likewise, those videos that Stacy and the LA group produced were of a quality that

George Powell could be proud. Powell-Peralta was a partnership that honored the quality of each other's creations.

For a skater, these videos are more than entertainment; they are training tapes. They are revelations of coordination and timing. The ollie, for instance, is a way of elevating a skateboard by means of a few flicks of the legs and feet, so as to be able to leap curbs initially, and thousands of variations. Just to see and experience the rhythm was key to picking up on what was evolving in the sport. So all you need is these simple devices; deck, trucks and wheels, and these videos to give you an entertaining lesson about how it's done. Just a few Powell-Peralta products are your keys to this worldwide amusement park; that, your evolving skills, and your willingness to take some lumps along the way.

Facilities had begun to share shop space with R&D in two garages with roll up doors. Chris' job was to devise methods of testing the company's products and various innovations. He had built a "guillotine" with ropes and pulleys that was designed to slam a weight down on a skateboard with adjustable force, to compare the breaking point of one contour or glue formula versus another. He would consult with the team riders on the individual shapes of their signature skateboards, and if we saw any of the Bones Brigade around our buildings in Santa Barbara they were there to see Chris about their deck, or to pow wow with Court across the street in the Art Department about their personal graphics, or touch base with Todd and George.

As soon as the Ver-Cal event was over, we had to remove the skating elements we had gathered there. That location was to become part of the expanding production of t-shirts and warehouse space. The big screenprinting autopress and drying oven were moved out of the Horton Building to the Ver-Cal Building. Facilities moved out of Chris' R&D shop, and took over the whole Horton Building. R&D doubled its space, and now Facilities had shop and yard space to spare. This was the beginning of serious volunteer ramp building efforts.

Chris Iverson had measured the space behind the Horton Building and had gotten permission to set up the Ver-Cal halfpipe there. One day he borrowed a huge forklift and a flatbed truck from somewhere and one by one carried the several sections of the halfpipe the 10 or so blocks from Ver-Cal to Horton. I jumped at the chance to be involved, and before long we had it set up, and I was able to get JW included. I must say that it was not at all difficult; everyone I dealt with there bent over backward to include JW and me in the fun. In particular, Joel, Peter, Ves, Chris Iverson, George Totten, and Todd Hastings; virtually everybody working there welcomed us and included us in every possible way.

That halfpipe was the first ramp I got to work on that was built by someone who knew what he was doing. Mike Taylor was a skater who had worked at Powell in the early 1980's and had built a number of ramps before I had done my first attempt in Puna. Mike had stashed a small halfpipe in a field in Goleta. He had left town with the Barfoot snowboard team and was living near Lake Tahoe. In his absence, his ramp had been hijacked for the Ver-Cal event.

Highlighting the wisdom of recycle-ability, the halfpipe had been built in sections, "modular" you might say, so that it could have many reincarnations. Every wood framed skateboard ramp since then we built in the exact same way: Between identical 3/4" plywood bulkheads with the prescribed radius, a ladder of 2" x 4" joists are end nailed or screwed with one edge flush with the arc. Two sheets of 3/8" plywood are curved into place and screwed to the joists. On top of that, a Masonite layer for the skating surface. This makes each section 4 feet wide.

It had originally been built for a skateboard shop in Goleta. When the skateshop closed, Mike Taylor moved it to a field nearby. While he was out of town, it was successively reborn as the Ver-Cal ramp, and then alternatively referred to as the Horton Ramp or the Cross-Bones Ramp, for the company's graffiti style logo that had been silk-screened just below the coping for the Ver-Cal event.

It fit neatly against a concrete block wall that was the backside of R&D's alley space, just outside of the Horton rear shop doors. We kept making improvements on it with wide rollouts with railings and netting to catch loose boards and a solid ladder.

In the Horton building, Facilities had a proper shop, and the company had big plans for it. Among the Facilities crew, there were a few that could perform rudimentary welding, but Joel was looking to bring somebody truly skilled aboard. I didn't know what good welding was until I'd seen a master at work. Mike Frazier showed up in about February 1988. Joel was really excited about hiring him. There were two things Joel liked about him: one, he was a great welder, and second, when Joel asked him why he left his last job, he answered that he had beat up his supervisor. I'm pretty sure that's what clinched the job for him. Joel had a kind of quirky orneriness like that. He appreciated directness and he was looking to assemble a sort of pirate crew with a broad range of skills. Unclear how I fit in.

Mike Frazier was a virtuoso of welding. He could do it all. Before long the shop had acetylene torches, arc welders, MIG wire feed welders, and TIG welders, which are wire feed welders for aluminum. He could make steel bend and move with great artistry and control, just by putting the torch here and there. He could make it dance. From time to time, he had to take a week off to work his side gig, which was to apply his skills to Department of Defense projects involving the need for high-tech welding with extreme precision. He couldn't say much about the projects except to report that most of the time there, he sat on the sidelines, but when the time came, his skills were the main event. In his side job, his compensation was astronomical, making 3 times what he made at Powell.

Another character in our shop was Andy Trapasso, though nobody ever called him that. He went by "Moose." It was a fitting nickname. He was about 6'-7", with a scraggly beard and in his former days had been an East Coast Hell's Angel. He had among his collection of videotapes, just about every skateboard video ever made, and a copy of Hell's Angels Forever in which he had a short appearance, ambling through one scene, just barely recognizable. You could tell it was him by the way he walked or kind of ambled along like a huge bowling pin about to tip over; teetering to one side and then the other.

Moose lived in Carpinteria, and when I realized he was taking the bus to work, I began picking him up for the ride to Santa Barbara with me. He told me the tale of how he lost his privilege to drive. It involved getting seven drunk-driving tickets on his Harley, in one day. The judge told him that when he got out of jail, he would never, ever get a driver's license again. Which was why he had been riding the bus.

Another story he told me was the time he had been riding his motorcycle down the New Jersey Turnpike, I think it was, at a high rate of speed when a pigeon smacked him square in the middle of his forehead. The helmet he was wearing cracked right in half, he was knocked unconscious, crashed, and spent over a week in a coma. He said he never was the same. He was a good natured and comical character when I knew him though the word was, one time, when he was in the role of a bouncer, he became irritated and had broken the offender's legs, somehow. I didn't really want to know how.

Another one of Moose's claims to fame, in my mind at least, was that he had been a roadie for the Grateful Dead for a while, and had accompanied the band on their tour to Egypt in 1978. That fact had a lot of resonance for me, because at the time, in the late 1980's, several of my closest friends were working in the Grateful Dead organization in Northern California. I had been a big fan of the band since I took part in building a stage for them to perform on in 1969, through my communal days in San Francisco in the early 1970's, and forever after.

The core of our Facilities crew was a contingent of people – Joel, Peter, Ves, – who had worked together before at the defunct Clenet, a custom fancy car builder company that had built cars for the Sultan of Brunei and the like. One of the key people in the art department, Nick Dinapoli, had been the designer at Clenet. The art department was in a former paint store across the street from the Horton building. Nick was the competent leader of the department; did the designs and shop drawings for the trade show exhibits, and oversaw the artwork on all the products, but the real creative genius over there was Court Johnson.

Court Johnson, in addition to being the main artist, was the company's unofficial shaman, it seemed. He was usually dressed in a white shirt and white pants and wore roller skates all day. He would roll through all parts of the factory, stopping here and there among the factory workers to administer his own sort of "tune-ups," in which he would find and release the aches and pains of repetitive motion, and occasionally perform a sort of psychological release as well. His technique was to have you stand upright, relaxed, with your arm held out to the side, parallel to the ground, and he would place his hand on your arm, and ask you these formulaic questions: about your health, about your love life, about your money issues; and invariably, when he got to the issue that was bugging you, your arm would involuntarily weaken and dip under the constant light pressure of his hand. Once he located the crux of your distress, he spoke these affirmations: admonitions concerning the issue. For instance, when your arm dipped on the money question, he would speak a short phrase that reminded you of all the times when you'd come up against the money problem before, and that somehow you'd gotten through it.

Then there was James. James Gardner was the company's computer whiz, authority in electronics and all things electrical. James lived about three quarters the way up the mountains behind Santa Barbara. His Mom owned the 50 acres or so at Flores Flats, most the way up Gibraltar Road toward the ridge of the Santa Ynez Mountains, surrounded by National Forest lands. This was way off the grid. James had grown up running around wild in the surroundings of their isolated homestead. He only wore shoes when somebody required it of him.

James was an early adopter of solar electric panels and deep cycle batteries, and by the late 80's had rigged up a Subaru with electric motors and golf cart batteries that he could commute down the mountain to work and make it all the way back up the winding road home on one charge.

The guy who turned out to be my closest buddy there was Gary Fowler. The name he preferred was "Ves," a name he had made up for himself. Ves had been part of the team at the Clenet auto works, like Joel and Peter. Ves had a variety of auto body related skills including painting. He was a surfer and also had surfboard-making chops: shaping, fiberglassing, and airbrushing. His brother was a well-known Santa Barbara surfboard maker. Ves had a number of personas, including that of a hippy. He always kept his hair long, never cut (as did Peter and Moose). He was a few years younger than me, about 40 at the time, and had the courage to take up skateboarding.

My own skateboarding experience began in the early 1970's. My friend Jim Hatch, aka "Steamboat" had been a bona fide beatnik. He was among the older bohemians that influenced me during those years and was part of our commune. He came up with some urethane wheeled skateboards in about 1971. We had a few experiences in the streets of San Francisco, including a certain paved playground out in the Richmond or Sunset district, I believe. It was composed of some asphalt terraces smoothly joined by asphalt slopes. It was quite fun, but I didn't take to skateboarding except in an occasional way.

Much later, in about 1975, we were all in Hawaii, and I decided to find out what my limits were. There was a long downhill two-lane road, Kahakai Blvd. leading down to the Hawaiian Beaches Subdivision to the home of a couple from our old communal family, Dick and Carol Latvala. Steamer and his wife Charlotte followed me in their rented car. I was picking up quite a bit of speed and I could see I was coming to a very rough stretch of pavement.

I hadn't developed the skills needed to stop, or even slow down. At the same time, I could see a car coming the other way and calculated that I would reach the rough spot about the same time as the oncoming car. I envisioned losing control and ending up under its wheels or as a bug on its windshield. I chose to bail out. Veering toward the right shoulder, I jumped off and tried to get my legs running as fast as I was moving, taking about three steps in 25 feet before my momentum had me hurtling toward the ground and rolling on the rocky rubble beside the road. Coming to rest in a jumble of lava rocks, ferns and popcorn Vanda orchids, I was one banged up haole. I had scrapes, cuts and bruises all over. Skating skills are gained incrementally, and the most avoidable injuries happen when you attempt more than you're ready for; my

Kahakai bailout is a prime example of that. Though I was always supportive of JW's skating, that slam ended my interest in getting on a skateboard myself until 1987, when I went to work for Powell-Peralta.

Anyway, getting back to Ves, we both began to learn to skateboard, but I soon found out, at this age, 44, with all the twists and turns necessary to skate, my body hurt even when I didn't fall down. I decided to hang it up, and stick to rampbuilding and taking pictures. Ves however, continued, and became skilled enough to skate all sorts of terrain including dropping in on the Horton halfpipe, and pulling it off. Over the following years, he continued to skate, and would often show up at work limping, tweaked or scraped in one way or another. He took a bad fall at Moguls above the Tea Bowl, damaging some internal organs. He had lot more willingness to take the lumps than me. He kept on skating. He was the crash dummy that kept reminding me I'd made a good decision. Finally, and most important, Ves was funny. He was a natural funnyman and clown. In fact, everybody in that whole Facilities brigade was funny. Ves was especially funny.

One of the first uses of our shop in the Horton Building was to build one of the big trade show exhibits for the ASR show in Long Beach. This particular exhibit was meant to showcase and emphasize Powell-Peralta's return to the use of seven plys of hard rock maple, after having experimented with something called "Bone-ite," where some of the plys in the lamination of our skateboards were of a high tech cellulose composite. In use, Bone-ite hadn't performed as well as expected, and the company wanted to highlight its commitment to return to the all-maple laminations. The theme of the exhibit, directed at action sports retailers, was gold: gold that the skateshop owners would reap selling Powell-Peralta products. Everything in the exhibit was to be gold. The walls were gold, the flyers were gold, the sales people were dressed in gold, and the video cabinet stands that it was my job to create, were upholstered in gold diamond pleated naugahyde. The centerpiece of the exhibit was a gold naugahyde pyramid, which I also got to build.

The pyramid was 8 feet tall and 4 feet square at the base. It was meant to be reminiscent of an old-time fortune telling booth. It had a viewing hole at eye level and a button you were to push when you looked in. Inside, we had rigged up the art department's mascot, a full size anatomically correct medical school skeleton named Rosie. She was seated on a simple seat painted flat black. When the button was pushed, a strobe light flickered inside and a buzzing solenoid animated her right hand so that it came up toward the eyehole displaying a hand of playing cards. The seven cards of the hand were seven plys of our hard rock maple, foretelling the future in seven ply maple skateboards.

Bone-ite was the only product failure I was aware of during my time at Powell. There were, however, occasional defects or defective runs in decks and wheels. One of our chores in Facilities was to destroy the defects before discarding them. The dumpsters at the company were regularly raided by local skaters, and efforts were made to put nothing usable in them, especially defective product.

The Gold pyramid signaled the end of the Bone-ite experiment.

In an odd chain of events, long after I left the company and moved up north, the gold pyramid ended up at the "Big House" in Macon, Georgia, where it has been since 1999. Long story.

Chapter 7 Moby Ramp

The next project was the main event, the reason we needed such a big shop, riverboat mechanic, truck driver, master welder and the varied skills of James, Ves and myself. We were to build the mobile ramp halfpipe for the 1988 summer tour. It was originally dubbed "Rad One," though I never heard anybody call it that.

I learned a lot from this project; skills and technologies that I had little or no former experience with; metal working, hydraulics, vacuum bag clamping, forklift driving, driving a team of horses, etc. Joel would go on and on with stories about his experiences on working barges and riverboats on the Missouri and Mississippi Rivers, where these enormous masses of floating steel tethered together with cables and huge pieces of hardware, turnbuckles and pulleys, would literally explode when being wrenched apart by the forces of a large body of moving water. Seeing that happen enough times, he had developed a sense of just how much stress and strain steel could take before bending and how much bending before breaking. With Joel, Mike Frazier and Peter on the project, engineering drawings were just the broad outlines, the "funny papers" they were obliged to start with, but departed from, and improved on, from day one.

A basic gooseneck fifth wheel trailer of a specific size was ordered from a local fabricator, and a brand new F-250 Ford pickup was purchased to pull it. From the first moment that trailer was backed into the yard behind the Horton Building, it was judged to be way too flimsy to survive the uses it was to be put to, the weight of what was going to be built on it, and the miles it would be driven around the country. Mike Frazier got busy upgrading or redoing all the substandard welding that it had come with, adding big steel gussets where necessary, the mountings for the heavy duty hydraulics and enormous hinges that would open and close it. Peter and Joel assigned various minor tasks to James, Moose, Ves, and me, including the creation of the compartment that would hold batteries for the hydraulic pump and trailer brakes, and after several weeks of this retrofitting, Ves gave it several coats of primer and finish coat of white paint. It was driven off to Carpinteria.

A custom boat builder in Carp had been hired to build the flatbottom and transitions; the skating surfaces. After about a week, the trailer was returned to the Horton Building with the flatbottom attached and our crew went to work on it again, installing the hydraulic cylinders and heavy pitman arms that would lower the transitions into skating position and lift them back up for travel. Back in the Carpinteria boat shop, a mold had been built, a "gel-coat" surface and many laminated ribs over the top of that, with vacuum bag clamping over the entire surface of laminations. The entire Facilities crew started showing up at the boat yard each day in Carpinteria. We were fortified by the R&D Department: Chris Iverson and George Totten. A newcomer, Sledge, had signed on specifically to be a roadie for the summer tour. The scheduled beginning of the tour was less than two months away, and there were many long days that ended well after dark. Being right there in Carpinteria, Moose and I had a short commute, and JW could bring a few of his pals by to see the spectacle after school.

The wings, the riding transitions, were very heavy, and it was necessary to rent a crane to hang them in position and suspend them there long enough to attach them to the trailer. Then, so the whole thing wouldn't be too tall to go under all the bridges we would encounter going across the country and back, the top sections of the transitions were hinged. All these different parts had to be assembled with as much precision as possible, cranes and fork lifts, and all hands doing something, drilling and tapping the huge pitman arm hinges, and the smaller continuous hinges for the top sections. Finally, one night, it all was together, and it could open and close by its own hydraulics. We were never sure the whole thing would work and when it finally did, nobody was more relieved than Joel. He deserves most of the credit for pulling it off. We did the best we could; he coordinated it all and earned our cooperation. I remember how happy he was when the wings were attached and the hydraulics were able to open and close them.

Still, the thing was together, but not quite

skateable. There were no rollout platforms at the top, and the smooth gel coat surface was too slick to skate, and when it got a little dewfall on it, it was like grease. You couldn't stand up on it: it was as slick as ice if it had any moisture on it at all. By the time we cleared out of the boat yard and got it back to Santa Barbara, most of us had taken at least one slam just trying to walk across the flatbottom.

Back in Santa Barbara, fixing that was the first priority. We set it up in the parking lot of the Ver-Cal building and hired a local sand blaster to make the surface grippy enough to skate. That evening as the sun was going down, Chris Iverson, George Totten and JW gave it its first test.

Time was growing short and summer was fast approaching. Mike Frazier was using a TIGG welder to create the tubular aluminum structure that would support the rollouts and complete the structure.

Still, we had to assemble the welded aluminum structure of the rollouts and railings, and attach coping, and figure out how it could be quickly set up and knocked down by two roadies.

Finally the day came when we were ready to go. The plan was to pick me up on the way through Carpinteria. I stood out there in front of our apartment building with my suitcase at the appointed time. The Rig didn't arrive. An hour went by. A while later someone showed up with the news. The ramp had made it less than three miles. Someone had neglected to torque down the lug nuts on one of the wheels of the mobile ramp, and it flew off on the freeway coming through Montecito. Joel had managed to keep the fishtailing trailer from crashing, and brought it to a stop on the shoulder, but the tire had been shredded. The tire was an odd size, having come with the trailer. It took way too much time to find a replacement, and began to look like we wouldn't make it to our first demo in El Paso, Texas. Finally we were on our way, with Todd Hastings driving the silver gray team van for our professional team riders. I wonder who picked the color of the van.

Chapter 8 Summer Tour 1988

When Jim Fitzpatrick came to work at Powell, about the same time I did, he already had a long history in the skateboard world, the longest in fact. He was one of those kids who made a skate out of adjustable roller skates, but by his account they had no peach box and handles, it was a hands-free skateboard from the beginning. He had been part of the professional skateboard world from its beginning, and was bringing his knowledge, contacts and his skills as a writer to work in the promotions department with Todd Hastings and Katy. He was going to join the Summer Tour in Texas to be the emcee for our demos and to be the supposed adult.

Joel took the wheel for the shakedown part of the trip, skirting the northern edge of Los Angeles and out across the Mohave Desert. He was working up the nerve to let me take the wheel of this rig. It had cost over $100,000 and the whole summer tour depended on it. He was showing me how wide to swing out into a right-angle corner "just like a team of horses" ...as if I knew what that was like. "Joel, I'm a Southern California surfer, a Northern California hippy, an East Hawaii jungle carpenter. What do you think I know about driving a team of horses?" I always remembered his advice, though, whenever I took a wide turn, "...just like a team of horses."

Somewhere coming across Arizona, we stopped for gas and there was a roadside curio shop next to the filling station. Sledge decided he'd just have to get himself some rattlesnake rattles and a cow skull; and just for good measure, a rattlesnake head with its mouth open and its fangs extended. He was so picky about the low quality and high cost of cow skulls that I don't believe he got one, but those rattlesnake parts he put on his bush hat and wore them there for the rest of the trip.

Sledge was a good name for him, especially in his present position. A "sledge" is old time circus slang for the workers that set up and tore down the big circus tents, using sledgehammers to pound in the huge tent stakes. He was short and muscular and built low to the ground ...you couldn't build a more perfect high speed downhill street skater, and only once on the whole trip did he demonstrate, since he had promised to keep it to a minimum. We couldn't afford an injured roadie–there were only going to be two of us after Joel went home. I think we were in Alabama and we had gotten the ramp set up when it started to rain. The ramp was not skate-able when wet, it just became too slick to even attempt. We took it down and drove on. We were riding out the rain squall in a nearby shopping center, when the rain stopped, the sun came out, and there was a very smoothly paved downhill ramp about 100 yards long, too choice for Sledge to ignore, and I was curious to see what he could do. Crouched low to the ground, on a board that was a bit longer than the standard of the day, he must have hit 35 mph by the time he gained full speed. At full speed he could throw it into a sideways slide that was the equivalent to slamming on the brakes, or what we used to call a brodie on bicycles. He had the skills that I had needed before I attempted the high speed run on Kahakai Blvd. back in 1975. What was I thinking?

Sledge had some very strong opinions about how certain restaurant food should be prepared, especially Italian. Since we were on the road and all our meals were in restaurants, there were several occasions in which he took the kitchen staff to task. I can imagine the waiter informing the chef "the gentleman with the skull on his shirt and a rattlesnake head on his hat wishes to offer a critique of the tortellini." We all had our quirks. Sledge was also doing a very smart thing; he was a collector of skateboard memorabilia and discontinued historic decks, like the aluminum and wood-laminated Quicksilvers and Quicktails (Powell's first skateboard decks). Since most of our demos took place near and under the auspices of a long established local skateboard shop, Sledge would quiz the skateshop owner about what old stuff he had in his backroom. He came away from most demos with something, usually several items of value. If he continued the pattern of collecting that he showed in those few months I knew him, somewhere there's a guy named Sledge sitting on a pile of treasures by now.

Our first demo was supposed to be held in El Paso, West Texas, but owing to our late start due to the wheel flying off in Montecito, and other delays, we didn't make it at the scheduled time. We drove off across Texas, which is the longest, most boring drive you ever took. Joel had foreseen the long hours behind the wheel, and had our rig and the team van outfitted with CB radios. We used them to keep in touch with Todd, Fitzpatrick and the team riders, but his favorite use of it was to amuse us all by telling lies to the truck drivers cruising along with us.

I hadn't experienced this before, but truck drivers chitchat with each other on their CB radios while driving along. They call out to each other, curious about the loads they are carrying and hazards up ahead including state troopers and weigh stations. Our odd rig had other truckers trying to figure out what we were pulling, and Joel would start spinning yarns. I don't think he ever told them what exactly it was. His two favorite stories were that we were pulling a secret DOD radar device: "We're not supposed to say what it is." Another was that it contained a bull elephant that we were taking somewhere for stud service. In the latter case, I'd make elephant trumpeting sounds and thumping on the sides of the cab to imitate our restless cargo. "Easy, big fella," Joel would say, then get back to his CB chatter.

Approaching the regional hub of Houston, we began to pick up the signal of a local CB enthusiast who had a setup in his house somewhere and he would amuse himself by insulting truck drivers passing through. "You truckers are the laziest fat sleazebags ever created. You call that work, sitting on your butts smoking cigarettes and watching the miles go by?" By and by he'd get somebody insulting him back, and claiming to know where he was, and threatening to pull a big rig up on his lawn and beat the hell out of him. Fun stuff like that. You've got to do something to occupy yourself driving across Texas.

Finally we arrived in Houma, Louisiana, outside of New Orleans, and put on our first show. For some reason, Fitzpatrick had to rent a car, maybe the van was in the shop, I forget why, but it was a Mercedes, and Joel asked to drive it after they had left the restaurant. I wasn't along. One of Joel's hobbies was to enter destruction derbies, and in that same vein, his first impulse with the wheel of a rental car in his hands, was to find someplace to get it off the ground: Meaning finding some railroad crossing or hump in the road, that hitting it fast enough would get the car airborne. It was the first time he ever had gotten the chance to catch air in a Mercedes.

That was Joel, and every once in a while, when we were in Louisiana, among the bayous and rivers, Joel would express a yearning for the life he had along the river as he was growing up in Missouri. In the evenings with thousands of acres of frogs croaking long into the night, with a far away look in his eye he would say, "A man could get a couple acres and just live on frog's legs."

Finally Joel felt safe enough to allow me to drive,

and he flew back to California, and Sledge and I continued on across Alabama and into Florida. By the time we had done a few demos I began to feel like I had indeed been transported into the movie, on a road trip with members of the Bones Brigade. In Florida, we did a demo near where Mike McGill's parents were living. They were in the process of moving from one residence to another, and we were enlisted to help them move. A year before, I was seeing these guys on the big screen. Now Sledge and I were helping their folks move furniture. Life is strange. At least mine is. Good though.

At a demo in a suburb of Atlanta, I think, we were set up in the parking lot of a shopping center, and a very small skater probably 5 or 6 years old, all padded up and helmeted with his skateboard, walked up to Rodney. Wasn't interested in an autograph. "Rodney, will you teach me how to ollie?" Rodney said, "OK, but later, come back later." The kid had gone straight to the top. Rodney was the creator and master of the flatland ollie. An hour or so later, kid comes back, "Rodney will you teach me how to ollie?" Rodney says, "I can't right now, but later, I'll teach you." I was keeping an eye out for this kid, wondering how was this going to play out. He came back again while Sledge and I were knocking down the halfpipe. I saw him get sent away again; Rodney was busy with the autograph line. Finally, we were all packed up, and the team was climbing into the van, end of a long day. The kid's there, "Rodney, will you teach me how to ollie?'" Rodney insisted on holding up the whole departure while he gave the young man a thoughtful, unhurried lesson in the art of the ollie, there alongside the open side doors of the team van, with half the Bones Brigade watching. They were real gentlemen, and always accessible to a fellow skater. I wonder where that kid is now, he was so determined. My guess is that in life, he found what he was looking for.

In South Carolina, Lance Mountain joined the tour and it so happened that a UPS shipment had arrived for us at the sponsoring skateshop. The package, from Santa Barbara, and was the first exposure of the new Lance Mountain model skateboard deck. Emcee-ing the whole affair over the PA from one of the rollouts, Fitz presented the deck to Lance with a great flourish and mock grandiloquent hype. Lance was clearly uncomfortable shilling for his own product. Though he shredded on cue as far as the skating went, I'm sure the hardest work he had to do was that kind of thing. Ray Barbee, and Jim Thiebaud had become part of the tour at that point.

At this same South Carolina demo, the only place we could set up the ramp was the narrow alley in front of the skateshop. This spot was especially dangerous for the spectators, since the spectators could not be kept at our normal distance. It was an easy guess where loose skateboards were most likely to go flying into the crowd. I stationed myself, Sledge, and two locals at the four spots where flatbottom meets transition at the edges of the ramp. Hands ready to catch loose boards, each of us stopped at least one board this way. Toward the end of the demo, sure enough, one of our pros, Brandon Chapman, dropping in, fell backward in a classic Wilson so that his skateboard launched right toward me. It took a bad hop, just clearing my fingertips, hitting me square in the mouth. Blood, blood, blood. One of my bloody teeth, root and all, landed grossly on the ramp.

The paramedics advised me to hold that knocked out tooth in my cheek, which I did, and at the emergency room they put it into a glass of milk while they stitched my lip, and cleaned me up. Then a friendly lady doctor wired that tooth right back into my skull, and sent me back to the skate demo in time to take down the ramp with Sledge, load up and make it to the next city on schedule, next day. You can catch a skateboard with your mouth, but it hurts, and you might not get all your teeth back.

Coming across the southern part of Virginia, a lightning storm was zapping the near highway; bolts on either side, bolts in front passing through a hissing patch of ozone steam where the rain had been a split second before. We fully expected to be vaporized any moment, but no, we arrived at the famous Mt. Trashmore skatepark as the clouds cleared.

In Virginia Beach, I think it was, it was one of the hottest, muggiest days we had ever set up our demo, and our pros were putting on their usual hell of a show. I remember how hard they were working, and Tommy Guerrero was in a state of exhaustion, I was afraid he was going to have heat stroke. Now, I have spent most of my life doing construction work all over coastal California and 10 years in Hawaii; I've witnessed a lot of people doing really hard work in the blazing sun. I never saw anybody working harder than Tommy Guerrero was working that day. He was flushed and panting and drenched with sweat after his run on the halfpipe. Still, he kept accommodating the endless fans asking for his autograph. At one point, I tried to keep them away, to give him a break, but he didn't want that. "Write my name on something? How can I say no to that?"

None of these Bones Brigade guys that I met had any kind of uptight attitude. They were genuine superstars of the skateboard, but gentlemen, good people, down to earth class acts. By the middle of summer, my part of the trip was over, and Peter Edwards flew out to take my place as driver/roadie for the rest of the tour. Sledge continued on with him for the whole grueling tour. I wouldn't have missed it, but I had had just enough. I returned to California with my spud wrench and exposed film.

Chapter 9 Meanwhile, back in California

In 1988, skateboard parks across the country were few in number. Astroskate in Texas, and Mt Trashmore, near Virginia Beach, were the only two we encountered on my part of the tour. There had been an era in the early 80's when a good number of parks had been built, but one by one they succumbed to two big bean counting problems. First, skateboarding is dangerous, and injuries are unavoidable. The liability of being responsible for what happens in a skatepark can be astronomical. As the insurance actuaries realized the facts of the situation, premiums grew until no skatepark could afford to pay them. The second problem was the parks didn't really make business sense, since there was little to sell, except access to an arena.

In an amusement park, you buy a ticket, somebody straps you in, and go on a ride; and it's safe, and you pay for every cycle of contrived thrill. In a skatepark, the skater creates the ride, and provides the vehicle, and powers it with his own energy and it's not safe. The safety is mostly a factor of the skater's skill, and self-awareness about his own limits. The park simply provides the topography. Most skateparks then, were never going to be money makers, and their creators had to be people who cared about skating and were willing to put up a sizable chunk of capital and real estate in order to launch something that would be big fun, but economically, a slowly sinking ship.

There weren't many skateparks by the time JW and I came into the scene, and it was our amazing good fortune that it was so (foggy day silver lining). If there were skateparks everywhere, the mobile ramp would have not been necessary, and there would never have been any reason for me to be driving across the country with the Bones Brigade. The first time we set up the mobile ramp on the road, it was in the parking lot of AstroSkate. It was an interesting oddity to the local skaters, but what they really wanted to see was the team tearing it up in their own familiar local skatepark, to watch them expand the possibilities of what could be done in the place they skated every day. In a world with skateparks everywhere, the pro tour wouldn't need Joel, Sledge, Peter and me, and this expensive cumbersome "portable" folding halfpipe.

Back in California, before the combination of "Rad One" and the team van, the company's professional demos were done using elements they could load onto the top of George Powell's old station wagon (gray). One of them was a launch ramp. It was an excellent launch ramp, but to the company it had become obsolete. Storage space was scarce. Joel asked me if I wanted it. Oh yeah. I loaded it in our little Datsun pickup and took it home.

This ramp became one of our favorite ways to entertain JW's cohort of Carpinteria skaters. It was large and heavy, but was just small enough that I could load it in the truck, by myself if need be, to take it around to various cul-de-sacs and parking lots, and the grounds of the High School. Once we got it out of the truck, of course, we could put it on a skateboard, and dolly it around easily.

A launch ramp is one of the basic devices to advance one's skating skills. It allows you to get your chops together to hit an element with enough speed to catch a little air and land, without the risks of dropping in on a halfpipe. Launch ramps can be too small, too tight a radius, and too lightweight to be hit at high speed without tipping it over or making it slide. The team launch ramp that Joel had given us was just right. The radius of the transition was 9 feet, the ramp itself was about 8 long, and it was too heavy to make skid by skating into it. You could launch and catch a little air.

Just as the small American towns where we did our demos, local skaters could put together a rudimentary temporary skatepark by collecting small launch ramps in a parking lot or playground to make a little scene. But there was no way to include a halfpipe into the mix. While there were plenty of places to go street skating, and launch ramps could make any flat pavement into an arena, there weren't a lot of places where you could go to experience vert skating. You needed a confluence of fortunate circumstances to bring a backyard mini-ramp into existence. Usually, it was a set of skateboard-enlightened parents with the property, the patience, and the money to put into their kid's obsession. It also took the willingness to stick their necks way, way out, as far as the liability for injuries. They were risking everything to make their kid's dreams come true. These kinds of parents were the heart and soul of skateboarding at a time when there were few retail or municipal skateparks to make that kind of skating accessible. This is known in skateboarding history as the era of "backyard ramps."

Typical of the state of skateboarding in the late 1980's, in Carpinteria, there was one such set of parents in the Delwiches. They had an avocado ranch on the backside of Rincon Mountain, with enough room for a mini-ramp, and the big hearts and courage to let a little skate scene happen. JW happened to be in the same classes at Carp High as their son, John, and by their junior year, JW and his usual skate buds were regulars up there. The basic halfpipe was small: 6-foot radius transitions up to 5½ feet high, not quite vert, 16 feet wide. JW got his photo in Thrasher, skating that ramp.

I don't quite know when we first came in to contact with "Team Effigy". It was probably when Mike Taylor came back from Tahoe to find his mini-ramp missing. He followed the clues and ended up in the back yard of the Horton Building. "Ah-hah!"

Santa Barbara has a long history in the skateboard world. Besides Powell's early aluminum and wood laminated Quicksilver Skateboards; Sims Skateboards and Barfoot Skateboards and Snowboards all were conceived of and being manufactured in the Santa Barbara area by the late 1970's. Of the loosely knit tribe that called itself Team Effigy that we got to know, most had worked for, or with, one or more of these skateboard companies, or were on their sponsored teams. Mike Taylor, Jeff Pixley, Robbie Olhiser, Mike Kresky and JB Baxter all fit into that category. They had been building ramps and putting on skate events long before JW and I showed up. By the time our efforts at Powell began to materialize in the SkateZone, they regularly volunteered as ramp builders (and clowns, of course).

Chapter 10 Slug Gone Bad

Still, our Carp brigade was limited to scenes around our local area.

The Bones Brigade odyssey as portrayed in Animal Chin was just for fun. These summer tours had some sense of that, but these guys were working; working really hard. I got to see them over an extended period of time, earning their keep. Back in Santa Barbara, you might think that there would be people working at the Powell manufacturing facilities who would resent the kind of money the professional riders were making. At this time, Tony Hawk was making over $100,000 a year, mostly from getting a cut of those hawk skull logo decks sold. I'm not sure that George or Stacy were drawing that much. But nobody among my friends at Powell begrudged them their situation at all. We all had steady reliable incomes doing jobs we knew we could continue to succeed at. The riders had to compete for the creds that would help them sell their boards, and they were doing something physically very dangerous. A major injury could happen at any moment, and up and coming talented younger competitors were getting harder to beat, and for those and innumerable unforeseen reasons, that record size royalty check they got last month might be their lifetime highpoint, the beginning of a downhill slide. What pressure. It was obvious that their fame and glory came with an uncertain future and great risks on many levels. Two of our professional skaters, Tony Hawk in vert contests, and Rodney Mullen in freestyle, were unbeatable for years, their competitors only shooting for second place. For each of them, that fact took a lot of the fun out of it. No reasonable person at Powell begrudged our pros' paychecks at all. Heck, no, those guys were risking it all, more power to them.

So I wouldn't recommend being a pro skater. It's hard work, with uncertain payoff. For a skater, it was probably a better deal to be a worker bee in the Powell factory beehive in Santa Barbara. Maybe the best deal of all was JW's deal: son of a bee in the Powell beehive. Sweet. Access all areas. No pressure.

I had gotten to know Chris Iverson around work and when we briefly shared shop space. Chris did the hands-on engineering of decks and wheels. We had collaborated on making elements for the Ver-Cal event, like the 100-foot rail slide, and the assembling, then the dismantling of the halfpipe and moving it to the Horton Building. I started bringing JW around on weekends and after school to help work on the ramp, and he got to know Chris and all my new friends.

The thing is that JW's skating skills were very strong and constantly advancing and he just happened to be the company's target demographic: 17 years old, avid skater and surfer, competent on street and ramp. While I had expected to be able to get JW skating equipment at a big employee discount, I was surprised one day when Chris started providing him with experimental decks. He never had to buy a skateboard again.

Beyond the measured technical testing methods like the guillotine, R&D needed products to be tested by skaters in their real world. The deal was that JW would go out and ride a new deck for a certain amount of time, then exchange it for another, reporting what he liked and didn't like about it. It also gave Chris a way to examine the effects of real life wear and tear. The shapes of skateboards were morphing rapidly during that period. Generally they started out mostly flat with a wide kicktail and a rounded nose. While we were there, Chris was experimenting deeper contour pressings for a number of different combinations of concavity. Finally it came to what seems obvious in hindsight; the double kick perfectly symmetrical deck with no nose and tail. JW was one of the very first to ride that shape.

JW got the same deal with wheels. Chris was tasked with creating and testing different shapes for the wheels: widths, diameters, edge contours. George was coming up with new formulas of urethane to provide skaters different choices of hardness or softness, springiness, durability. All these products needed to be tested.

Chris started joining our skate safaris. He knew all the cool ditches and parking lots, and as we ranged farther and farther south, he was able to gain us entry into some places we could never have gotten to.

After I went to work at Powell, I realized I didn't need a pickup anymore, so I traded it for a dark blue Dodge station wagon we called "Midnight." With a super dependable easy to work on slant-six engine, it was our bus to all these skate adventures. I was the driver, a scout, and the photographer. The early trips took us to the San Fernando Valley, to known locations of ditches and banks; an abandoned house with an empty swimming pool in Sepulveda, and on east out toward San Bernardino to Mt Baldy Dam.

The destination was a big spillway that had a very skate-able full pipe coming out of the base of the dam. It was about 20 feet in diameter. You had to cross a wide dry river bed and climb through some fences to get down into the big rectangular drainage channel, then walk maybe 75 yards up to the full pipe.

One day I was up there, I forget who was along that time; it could have been Chris, Ves, Jesse, Nashia, Judd and JW of course. I was sitting there changing the film in my camera, when "SMACK!!! WHIZZzzzzzzz." Something hit the side of my leg and buzzed off. It really hurt. I pulled down my Levi's to get a look at the spot I was hit on my left leg, just above the knee. There was a welt on the side of my leg, puffed up with a bloody spot in the middle. We had seen some kids with a .22 rifle out plinking when we were crossing the riverbed. We started shouting for them to stop shooting, their ricochets were hitting us, and after awhile they poked their heads over the fence above the full pipe and said, "Sorry, oops and goodbye."

You know, sometimes I think I'm too easy going. It wasn't until we were sitting in a restaurant in Uplands a few hours later that I felt any anger toward those kids. If that had hit me or someone else in the side of the head or the eyeball, it would have been a far more serious event. It wasn't, and I had just laughed it off. Now, the swollen jelly donut throbbing, I realized; the normal reaction would have been to get mad.

Looking through the photographs of that day, there was an odd phrase and cartoon in the graffiti on the wall: "Slug Gone Bad." Yep.

Chapter 11 The Noodles Tours

On most of our skate safaris nobody got shot. We got out the map of Southern California to chart our expeditions. A tangle of red and blue arteries depicted the endless maze of freeways. Chris referred to them as “noodles.” That sort of stuck; we began to refer to our weekend safaris as “Noodles Tours.”

We could take one-day forays to the San Fernando Valley, and on east to San Bernardino. Also known as San Berdoo. Southern California is basically a desert that comes down to the ocean. It pipes a lot of its water down from the Sierras in giant aqueducts. Most of the year it is arid, but when rain comes, it can easily become a deluge. To deal with that cyclical predictable disaster, the whole landscape of these inland valleys is criss-crossed with flood channels. The massive concrete flood control projects have no purpose whatsoever when it’s not raining. Or do they? Like the Mt Baldy dam, Puddingstone Dam, various diversion dams, and innumerable ditches and urban creeks, they are bone dry 95% of the time, smoothly troweled and skateable.

Within our one-day range we could make it out to Baldy and the nearby Uplands Skatepark. Uplands was one of the few skateparks to survive during this era of liability concerns. It was a quite an elaborate complex of outdoor concrete elements, a long slowly sloping halfpipe, several deep pools, and a full pipe. Concrete skating surfaces are obviously less forgiving when a skater falls, and skaters would prefer plywood and Masonite to land on if they had their druthers. The advantages are economic. First of all, concrete is far more durable, and can be built outside where it can survive in the rain and sun. Ramps made of wood inside or out are in a constant state of decline and will need maintenance. At minimum they will need to be periodically re-skinned with Masonite.

At one point we made a noodles road trip to Northern California. That trip it was Chris Iverson, Ves, George Totten, JW and me. We hit what spots we had heard about; the drained Casting Ponds in Golden Gate Park, Derby Park in Santa Cruz, a well-known concrete snake run in a public park, a glimpse of the future.

By then, my old buds Dick and Carol had moved back to the mainland also, and parted ways. They had both found jobs in the Grateful Dead organization. We looked in on Dick, at home in Albany with his second wife, Christie, picked up some tickets and made it to a Grateful Dead concert at the Oakland Coliseum, where we raged to the early morning hours, and got back to SB about dawn.

But the best Noodles tour ever was our Grand Tour of Southern California. This particular trip touched most of the bases in Southern California. That trip it was Chris Iverson, George Totten, JW and me.

The first stop was at Eric Sanderson's house, where he had a six-foot high spine ramp in his backyard. At first it was just Eric and we noodlers. After awhile Lance Mountain showed up with his son, Lance Jr., about 4 years old. I admired the clean carpentry of the ramps. Somebody with high standards had put this together.

After we left there we drove down to Tony Hawk's house in the northern part of San Diego County. Tony was home, but was laid up with a knee injury. We went in to visit him a little bit in the living room where he was propped up with his leg packed in ice. After that we had his backyard spine ramp to ourselves. It was my good fortune that Tony's Dad, Frank Hawk showed up. We had a little conversation about ramp construction and in particular, bowl corners.

Next morning we showed up at Mike McGill's skatepark in Carlsbad, north of San Diego, before it opened and the boys again had a skatepark to themselves. Mike's place had an array of wood ramps with two vert ramps at right angles to each other and a gentler halfpipe, all built outdoors. It's dry enough down there for them to survive outside five years or so. Like everywhere else, Mike's park helped pay the bills with a skateshop and refreshments.

Later we drove down to Tijuana for the last destination on our road trip. We parked on the US side and walked across the border. I wasn't taking Midnight down there. We got in a cab with our skateboards and the driver already knew where we wanted to go. Just up the hill from the center of town there was an outdoor set of concrete bowls and snake runs that took up a quarter acre vacant lot, street to street. An enterprising kid by the street asked for a dollar or two to let you in, and sold sodas too. Mike McGill said he might join us there, and sure enough he did.

That was our most memorable Noodles Tour, like living in the movie.

Chapter 12 The Lemon House 1989

Like I said, when I started working at Powell, the demand for the company's products was so strong that the factory couldn't keep up. My hiring was part of the expansion of the Facilities crew, which was needed to continue modifying new leased space around the Gutierrez street neighborhood. Each time we acquired a new building, there was machinery to be moved into it, set up, powered, vented, etc. It seemed cumbersome to have all these different buildings at the time.

It's easy to assume when your sales are enjoying rapid growth, that it will continue. George could envision the need for even more space in the near future and was running out of possibilities down there on Santa Barbara's Lower East Side. He found a building out near the Santa Barbara Airport in Goleta that had been an enormous lemon packing facility, over 180,000 square feet, quite a bit more space than we were currently occupying. It was going to be "PCHQ:" Powell Corporation Headquarters. There would be expanded room for all departments all under one roof. Sales, screenprinting, huge woodshops for the decks, big urethane department, massive warehouse space, huge Facilities shop in the basement, big penthouse art department, retail factory outlet store, theater, and, we just might have enough extra space to build an indoor skatepark.

The factory complex was in need of extensive remodeling, since we weren't going to be packing lemons. It would be six months or so before the company could move into it. It was composed of eight 60' x 150' dark and musty bays, and two high ceiling 150' x 150' bays with a 50' x 100' penthouse on top of the two. It needed skylights for natural light in all the bays; loading docks around in back; new entrances into the parking lot; a new façade along La Patera Lane for the offices and retail space; new pavement all the way around, perfect for skating. And, of course, the whole thing would have to be painted inside and out in multiple tones of gray.

One more thing the property had. Next to the front gate there was a separate 1000 square foot building that had been the Lemon Association's offices and accounting department. It was offered that JW and I live there while the factory remodeling went on, to be an on-site presence, security and company rep on nights and weekends when the construction crews were gone and go to my regular job at the Horton Building during business hours. We had been living in a studio apartment in Carpinteria. JW was in his senior year in high school and had his own car, a red 1969 Dodge Dart. It was about a 25-mile commute from the factory to Carp High. No problem.

The building wasn't set up like a house. It had a counter facing the front door, a huge open room that once had rows of people working at desks, which we used as our living room, a small glassed-in corner office that became JW's bedroom, a big bedroom for me whose windows faced the La Patera Lane entrance to our main parking lot, a couple of half baths, no shower, no kitchen. It had a walk-in vault that was used as a fire-safe storage for company records.

I built a shower, we set up a rudimentary kitchen, and it was our pad for the next two years while the PCHQ building was being completed. We first helped build a skatepark in the parking lot outside our window, and then moved it all inside to form the beginnings of the indoor SkateZone, right across the driveway.

When JW was younger, he would spend part of his summers with his grandparents on the mainland. They took him golfing a lot, and the kid was pretty good at it. He got pretty obsessive about drawing pictures of golf courses, usually a view from the tee-off point with contours, doglegs, sand traps and the putting green off in the distance. After he got hooked on surfing and skateboarding, the subjects of his drawings were surf spots with breaking waves or ramps and skateparks, real or imagined. Starting with the Animal Chin ramp, he made renditions of all the ramps we'd experienced in our travels. We covered the walls of the Lemon House with those drawings.

Chapter 13 Vancouver

There's got to be some love stories in this somewhere, and I watched a sweet one begin to unfold there in front of the Horton Building. Jeannie had been working in production, I think. She was one of the two girls who worked at Powell who could actually skate. She popped in to use the sink and mirror in our restroom. She was all excited. She was going on a lunch date with Chris Iverson. He came walking down the sidewalk on Gutierrez St. and she skipped out to join him. I never saw either of them with anybody else after that.

Somewhere about this time we took a trip to Vancouver to complete our West Coast exploration of the Powell-Peralta empire. At first, I think, it was JW, Chris Iverson, George Totten, and myself. We landed in Seattle and took a rental car across the border. Somewhere along the way, Jeff Pixley and Jeannie joined up with us.

The Vancouver skateboard scene was an eye-opener. In Canada, when a skater got seriously injured, he went to the doctor; in California, he got a doctor, a lawyer and an insurance company. With universal health care, injuries are just taken care of without activating a chain of for-profit middlemen.

Seeing the North Vancouver Snake Bowl was like looking into the future, down to the specifics of the signage. It was a very well designed concrete snake run in a public park that slalomed down a gentle slope ending in a bowl. Like Derby Park in Santa Cruz, this is a model for outdoor municipal skateparks. Minimal maintenance, free admittance, skate-at-your-own-risk unsupervised concrete terrain dedicated to skating is the perfect recreational, economic and legal choice. After the initial expenditure for construction, it costs nearly nothing. Just like a basketball court, a soccer field, a horseshoe pit or any number of recreational activities, you can't charge money for its use. By the time skateboarding became a mainstream sport in California, it was only natural that public parks would accommodate skaters in exactly this way.

The Canadians were way ahead in another respect. There were three outdoor public skate parks around the city but they were useless in the frequent rain, and the occasional snow and ice. To provide northern skaters with a place to go in any weather, Kevin Harris had built two indoor "Skate Ranches." Kevin was a freestyle pro for Powell, part of the Bones Brigade. He had been touring with the team the early part of my '88 Summer Tour. In each location, he had filled the room with whatever collection of halfpipes large and small he could squeeze into the space. The larger of the two was the forerunner of what we would end up building at PCHQ. It had a series of progressively taller halfpipes butted right against each other with a common flatbottom, all the way up to full vertical, so that all skill levels could find something they could skate and choices to challenge their limits.

It's hard for a skatepark to pay for itself, but he was making it work somehow with adjoining skate shops and cafés. He had a photo ID and membership system for his regulars, and a rate structure for all comers, which was copied for SkateZone.

Chris Iverson and Jeannie, Totten, Pixley, JW and I at that time comprised an all-Powell entourage and we got the royal treatment at the skateparks backstage after hours, before hours, anytime.

Displayed on the walls were photographs of the Skate Ranch framing during construction. I love that look of a skeletal skatepark, right before it gets the skin on It. I can see the work of the carpenters' hands. I was beginning to feel the joy of our upcoming build out of the SkateZone, the pleasure of filling an entire room with skate ramp skeletons, committing the space to a zone for fun.

We got the complete picture of how a world could be with skateboard parks. Just the issue of perceived liability was keeping a lid on all the possibilities in California. It would take some legal workarounds for the SkateZone to exist.

Chapter 14 MacKenzie Park SkateZone

"Skateboarding is not a crime," read the bumper stickers. As the popularity of the sport grew, more and more property owners, schools and businesses were putting up signs prohibiting it. The Company was increasingly promoting a public skatepark in some form, somewhere in the company's home turf. We could see all the signs that said "skateboarding prohibited." How about some signs that said "Skate Zone," signs designating a place where skating **is** permitted? Encouraged, even.

The powers that be at Powell–George, Chris and Fitz probably–came up with the idea of a "Skate Zone" Demo. By then we had quite a bit of collective experience putting on public shows across the country with our mobile ramp as the centerpiece. Invariably, in every town we appeared on some big parking lot, the locals would transport their portable launch ramps down to the scene and a momentary skatepark would exist for that one afternoon.

Here in our own hometown, the Company could provide our own collection of skating elements, and the R&D/Facilities crew got to work creating them. This is the point where our rampbuilding took off. Up to that point, our work on the Crossbones Ramp had been mostly a volunteer effort. With Powell putting on its own local event, all the resources of Facilities and R&D were used on company time. Mike Frazier's welding skills gave us perfect coping; the company paid for all the materials, and we had a full gallery of pieces to build.

MacKenzie Park sits up against a hillside on upper State Street. It was part of the site of a WWII temporary hospital they made into a park when I was in high school. It has a big grassy field, a couple of baseball diamonds, basketball courts and a big parking lot surrounding the Army Reserve Recruiting Station on the corner. Everything we needed for a deluxe event.

We set up the mobile halfpipe on the lawn. In the paved basketball courts we scattered an array of launch ramps and sections of the railslide from the Ver-Cal event, and a freestanding two-sided wall ride that turned out to be the most popular element. A steep hillside on the south edge of the park made for excellent viewing of the whole spectacle. Stars of the Southern California skate scene who were pros for other companies showed up to support the cause; including skateboarding's own DJ, Skatemaster Tate.

Thousands of skaters and curious pedestrians spent the whole afternoon there, enjoying the free form spectacle. By early evening we had to remove all the skating elements.

With the temporary skatepark torn down and hauled away, many skaters moved on to the nearby Laredo Plaza parking lot and did cause some problems. That's just the point, without a zone for it; skaters practice their sport on the world at large.

The MacKenzie Park SkateZone was a big success; proving skateboarding events are not anarchists' riots, just young athletes having some fun. The city fathers were starting to see the light. Fitzpatrick was making sure that in the halls of government, and in municipal parks departments statewide nobody would miss the calculation: a basketball court, for example, might entertain a few people, maybe 10 at once, but most of the time there's nobody there. A baseball diamond, with all its need for maintenance and grass mowing, likewise sits most of the time unused. But a skatepark is used almost constantly.

Chapter 15 PCHQ Jamming

The night we tore down the MacKenzie park set-up, Facilities hauled it out to the new PCHQ building where one of the huge bays in the back had been swept out to have a skate jam for all the visiting pros who showed up to support the SkateZone idea. By dark the party began arriving. Moose stood by the door checking the creds of those trying to enter. The bay had been swept as carefully as possible but the old concrete was disintegrating and as the skating went on a hazy cloud rose to give the room a fogged look. About half of the lights we rented didn't work so the room had a dim and surreal look to it. Hundreds of skaters had found their way in.

The band was loud and the beer was free and the most popular elements to skate were the four small transitions that had supported the wall ride. They had been placed side by side against the huge concrete wall at the south end of the bay and the skaters were taking long high speed runs at them, going up one set of two, carving the wall and back down on the other two. The higher they got, they reached a level where some metal brackets had been crudely torched off the wall, and skaters were starting to get ripped by them. Skateboarding tip: Don't have jagged pieces of steel protruding from the vertical skate surface, in a dim and dusty warehouse in the middle of the night with free beer.

Everybody had fun, though…and their wounds all healed.

After the MacKenzie Park event, we had all these portable skate elements, enough to have a small skating area in the PCHQ parking lot, right outside JW's window. The powers that be envisioned amateur skateboarding contests that could be held there, and sure enough they had quite a few of them, called Quartermaster Cups and Am Jams.

Like surfing, skating to me was an existential pastime: a personal flowing kinetic sensual dance. Competitive skateboarding transforms that dance into an entertaining spectacle with its motivation to excel. The contests were an excuse to sponsor public events, make a scene, and share the parking lot Zone with a wider group of skaters. Who won, who lost? I don't know. I hope nobody lost.

The contests were designed as perks for Powell-Peralta dealers to bring their local amateur teams for an event at the factory, show everybody a good time and for the company to spot the up-and-coming skaters soon to turn pro.

JW entered one of those contests. He could skate at the level of Powell's own amateur team, but he didn't care for the competition and the pressure. He was already getting all the perks our amateur riders were getting, and more. We had no way to lose and he had more ways to win. Living on the property there, JW was spending more and more time helping us build stuff, and of course drawing pictures of what we had built, but now he was drawing pictures of stuff before we built it, becoming indispensible in the design process. We got to build additions to the topography before each new event, sometimes on company time. I remember the grand funbox we stayed up late into the night to get finished for the next day's contest. By the time we moved the SkateZone inside, JW was the key player in everything we built.

Chapter 16 Moby Ramp II

Two new guys got hired to beef up the Facilities crew for the upcoming factory move. They were friends Artie Corradi and Doug Adamski. I didn't know them before, but it doesn't take long for Deadheads to recognize each other, and these guys were avid. With my connections to the Grateful Dead ticket office, I could come up with tickets at the last minute for shows in California.

I remember when Artie first got his job at Powell; it was the second or third day, and he got a flat tire on the way to work, driving over from his sister's place in Ojai. The last thing he wanted to do at this point was to be late to work. Peter, our foreman, showed a gruff exterior to newcomers, and he had been putting Artie and Doug to the test. Artie got a flat tire somewhere on the 30-mile trip over Casitas Pass Road from Ojai to Gutierrez Street in Santa Barbara, and continued to drive until every shred of the tire was gone, and still he continued to drive down the back roads along foothills of Carpinteria and Montecito until he arrived at the Horton Building, right on time with the rim of one wheel a molten, smoldering ruin. Kept the job, though. That's how I'll always remember Artie.

His buddy Doug Adamski was overqualified for the miscellaneous unskilled tasks he was given, but he needed a job at the moment and was happy to find himself in a place where Grateful Dead was spoken. He could skateboard a little bit and I watched him struggle to get his chops together, but like me, he was getting banged up and never got committed to it. He left Powell after we had moved the company to its new digs, but we've stayed friends ever since.

The mobile ramp had been a big success in its first incarnation. The combination of the gooseneck fifth wheel trailer and the Ford F-250 had served its purpose, but just barely. It was too lightweight. The decision was made to cut off the gooseneck, and replace it with a standard pintle hook and lunette ring, so that a larger truck could pull it. It also needed a beefier set of axles with standard size tires we could replace anywhere.

A larger truck was a good idea for a few other reasons. The company bought a Peterbilt with a 20-foot box and a lift gate. The big box could be used to carry a decent collection of smaller skate elements for our demos, and quite a bit of our product as well. Big graphics of a Powell dragon were applied to the sides of it.

The ramp would just barely fit under the doorway of the Horton Building and it was squeezed inside so that Mike Frazier could do the cutting and welding for a different type hitch. Before you knew it, the gooseneck was cut off and lying on the ground and the tang of a beautifully welded lunette ring was integrated with the structure of the trailer in its place. James rerouted the lines for the hydraulic cylinders that operated the ramp's wings into a new compartment for the batteries and hydraulic pump. Once it was all put together, Joel was able to maneuver the rig out of the building with a forklift and into the backyard, across from the CrossBones halfpipe. For a short while, we had two usable halfpipes in the back lot.

Outside, we went to work on the ramp itself. A problem with the mobile ramp on the '88 Tour was that the 4 foot wide rollout platforms had to be lifted up and down from the aluminum tube struts and placed inside the folded up ramp on the flatbottom for travel. This was part of the grueling process of setup and tear down. It was determined that if we had a little narrower rollouts, they could be attached to the hinged part of the transitions, so that they would fold up and down as one piece, saving us the work of taking them off.

We came up with a structural design that would have narrower rollout platforms fold down against the convex outsides of the ramp. Once I had completed the woodwork, Ves used his skills to fiberglass the entire new structures for strength and waterproofing. Mike Frazier rebuilt the tubular aluminum struts that supported the whole works, and the railings on the rollouts. Ves sprayed the new steel with primer and white automotive paint like the rest of the chassis. We finally attached Lexan curbs to the edges of the skating surface to prevent loose skateboards from whacking somebody in the face...again. With that, mobile ramp version 2.0 was ready to hit the road.

With the new configuration, as a truck and trailer, one man could do the whole thing. And since the bigger rig required a commercial driver's license, Peter Edwards became the sole ramp master. In this capacity, he could drive anywhere in the country and set up a little skatepark, single handedly…and did, for years thereafter.

That was one of the last major projects we did at the Horton Building. Pretty soon Facilities would be consumed with the moving the entire company to Goleta.

Chapter 17 AutoCad

JW devised a style of drawing skate ramps, with two-point perspective and a color code that showed you instantly what was transition and what was flatbottom or rollout. We put them up around the main room of the Lemon House. He had made quite a gallery of them.

The skateboard company had a guy whose job it was to make engineering drawings for all the plant's needs. He had a computer set up to make them, with AutoCad software. "CAD" meaning "computer assisted drafting." I was fascinated by the prospect of learning how to do it. I found that there were classes at the City College, and signed up.

The prerequisite was a class in basic drafting. I hadn't taken a drafting class since junior high school, 1957, and I didn't think I would gain much from it, but I did. It was a simple idea about line thicknesses: How to make the image pop off the page and the dimensions not clutter what you're seeing, but be there for reference.

I was taking courses at SBCC anyway and guessed there might be something I could glean from their engineering program. I signed up for the prerequisite Eng.101, Introduction to Engineering. I was surprised by the insights I gained from that course too. One of the assignments was to interview a working engineer and write a report about it. At the time, Powell had an engineer named Ralph who was signed on to design the utilities in the new manufacturing facility: routing the power conduits and compressed air lines and dust collection systems, stuff like that. I took him out to lunch at an outdoor café on Milpas Street about 4 blocks from the company's neighborhood.

His college degree in marine engineering emphasized ship construction and all the systems that needed to be routed compactly through large vessels. He had expected to be a maritime engineer, but after graduation he had gone to work at the Ford plant that made F-100 pickups. He said he had worked in a large office space with lots and lots of other engineers. He said the place had an excitement to it, like in those old movies of a big city newspaper office where somebody bursts in with a scoop..."Stop The Presses!" Only in the engineers' office, it was more like a bingo parlor when somebody would jump up from the drafting table with a breakthrough..."Eureka!" Poring over the minutiae of every detail of the truck's construction, they were working to redesign a part or system of parts that would accomplish the same function in a way that could be manufactured more cheaply. When an engineer had such an insight that would save even 50 cents a truck, he would earn his pay for years to come with that one flash. Ford was going to build millions of them. Who knew engineering could be exciting?

As we sat there next to the busy noontime traffic on Milpas Street, he started pointing out the Ford pickups driving by that were the model years he worked on. It was comical how many there were, sometimes two at a time; side by side or going the opposite direction. Soon I was able to pick them out and we kept a running total through the course of lunch. There must have been over 30 of them.

Anyway, back to drafting; besides drawing the plans for the small houses I was building myself, I had made some of my living in Hawaii making permit drawings for people who had gotten in trouble with the County Building Department. Typically, a young hippie couple had bought a piece of jungle, hacked a clearing and the put up a one-room cabin with a shed roof. After a long time, if somebody complained or by some random happenstance, a building inspector would happen by, it would get red-tagged to the great distress of the young pioneers. I was the fixer who could imagine their shack as part of a larger design that would meet the codes, that was simply unfinished, and make the necessary drawings so that everything was in order for the County. The permit would be granted, and for the price of my simple drawings and the regular permit fee, the homesteaders could relax and get back to their real life. Nothing needed to be done to the building except staple up the permit card, and the building inspector would drive by and smile and wave aloha. Its bureaucracy appeased, it was known that the County would leave you alone for five years or so, before insisting on progress, if they ever did. No law against running out of money before you finish the whole thing.

In those days I could do my drawings on 11" x 17" Clearprint graph paper, and make Xerox copies for the building department. A mistake or a changed idea would require a lot of erasing or starting over. When I saw AutoCad in action at the Powell factory I knew I had to take the leap into the computer age. Drawings could be done with such easy precision and revised so painlessly that I had to drop in. I took the classes at SBCC and bought my first computer. It was a 486 DOS machine, which was pretty advanced for that day, built from scratch by CompuCad, a local company, especially for computer drafting, with a digitizing pad and a pen plotter, and I was tooled up.

I was able to make professional looking drawings for factory remodeling projects, and amuse myself with artsy ideas that were made easy by the technology, like my PPP Triple Manifold, a variation of the Triple Encabulator Tuned Manifold, a well-known optical illusion. Few people looked at it long enough to get it. It was taped to the inside of my office window. At a glance it just looks like a standard Powell Peralta triple p logo.

Of course, my best use of the setup was to map out the indoor SkateZone as it began to take shape. At first it was the collection of portable ramps from the MacKenzie park demo, plus the growing list of fun-boxes and elements from our parking lot SkateZone events. As time went on, new elements were created, and existing pieces were rearranged. I made a precise floor plan of the building and kept updating the locations of the elements.

Chapter 18 Bay of Cubes

In my world, new friends literally pop out of the woodwork. Doug Hechter is an over-the-top craftsman and project manager (and Deadhead) who was hired to construct the huge bay full of cubicles for all kinds of our desk workers; each with a niche for a computer monitor, some file cabinets, electric outlets and phone lines. Clusters of 4 desks stood on short concrete platforms. Before the slab had been poured, a network of channels and conduits had been laid down so that all the electrical, phone and computer cables would all come up in the center of each workstation without wires on the floor.

George Powell had designed the whole arrangement down to the details of the walnut trim, and the cloth covered panels; gray of course, and the carpet, gray also.

It was an enormous project of cabinetry, 48 workstations, and Doug Hechter was brought onboard to pull it off. Hundreds of identical pieces of plywood needed to be cut, rabbeted and dadoed with precision. Thousands of feet of walnut trim needed to be milled with bullnose and a channel, then precisely cut and mitered. Hundreds of panels needed to be stretched with padding and cloth and installed.

Doug set up his shop in one of the future production bays that wasn't in use yet. He needed a lot of space for his staging area. He enlisted some of us Powell employees to help with the volume of tasks: Jamie Johnston from the woodshop, George Totten from R&D, me and Ves from Facilities. We had shop tools, spray booths and a great variety of skills.

By the time Doug had finished and moved on, we had become good friends. Years later he would connect me with some truly exceptional projects; exotic mansions, I'd have to call them. He had been part of a communal tribe in the woods of the Navarro Ridge, in Mendocino County, back in the 1970's. Long after I left Powell and moved to Northern California again, I got to meet and work with remaining members of his free spirited commune on a palace of recycled redwood near Sebastopol in Northern California. They in turn have become close friends of mine and adventures with them continue to this day.

Anyway, the cubicle bay was finished, and JW and I were living there in the Lemon House. Besides doing my regular job in Facilities, I had to keep an eye on the comings and goings of everyone and anyone after hours, at night, and on weekends. I couldn't be awake all the time so we began to enlist some of our production workers to spend the night inside the building for a little extra pay. There had been some pilfering of materials during the construction phase that wasn't too concerning. But one was an inside job where somebody working for one of the subcontractors left an extension ladder up the 20-foot side of the building so he and his buddy could gain access to the unlocked doors on the roof after hours. Our man in the building heard them come in and fearlessly raced up to confront them. Hearing someone coming, the intruders ran back out on the roof and were scrambling down the ladder, when our man emerged with a carbine in his hand and yelling in Cambodian. They made it to the bottom of the ladder without breaking any bones and raced off terrified in their pickup truck. I didn't know he was going to bring a gun; it was never discussed.

Since we didn't want anybody to get shot, and the unfinished building began to be occupied by departments whose areas were completed, a private security company was hired to provide a watchman to patrol the exterior for an 8 hour period at night, so I could get some sleep.

The building was finished enough that most production bays were up and running, the indoor SkateZone was half finished and all departments like Personnel, Sales, Promotions, Management, that had been scattered about our Gutierrez St. complex were now all housed in Doug Hechter's Great Hall of Cubicles. The building had an elaborate alarm system that would show on a panel the opening and closing of every door, of which there were over 100. But the building was not finished, and the alarm system was not operational. At closing time, I would make my rounds, locking all doors to the exterior, then settle in for the evening at the Lemon House.

While the building was in this state, I got a report that someone had gotten into a petty cash box, in one of the drawers in the cubicle area. It had happened once before, but they hadn't told me, thinking it was a mistake or a one-time pilfering during the day. The second time, I was told, and they had determined that it must have happened after hours. The third time James–our computer tech, AV guy and electrician–and I took action.

There was a conference room on a mezzanine level that overlooked the maze of cubicles. The familiar full size photographic cardboard cut outs of the team were placed up there to provide cover for our video camera, set to record a frame every second on videotape. James set up the security camera to run continuously all night and rigged a silent alarm to the drawer where the cash box was kept. When triggered, a remote phone silently dialed the phone next to my bed at the Lemon House and played a recorded message.

It didn't take long, the first or second night we had the trap set, the phone woke me up. "Break-in at Powell Headquarters… Break-in at Powell Headquarters," in my own voice. Sure enough, we got a bite. I called 911 and explained the situation; there was a burglary in progress. They said they would send out a Deputy Sheriff.

I got dressed, got my keys and went out to the street. In less than a minute, I could see the black and white patrol car turn off Hollister Ave, about 300 yards away. I waved my flashlight in that direction and he switched off the headlights as he came toward me. I met the deputy at his driver's side window, quickly explained the plot and what part of the building the silent alarm came from. He climbed out and retrieved his dog from the back seat.

We quietly walked to the front door that opened almost directly to the cubicle area and entered. The deputy shouted, "SANTA BARBARA SHERIFF'S DEPARTMENT, STAND AND SHOW YOURSELF!" ...Silence. The German shepherd was getting excited. There was a tiny squeak of a desk chair. He loved this game. Even without anything our senses could pick up, he already knew where the bad guy was, by sound and smell. This would be easy. Silence. The deputy shouted, "I'M GOING TO RELEASE THE DOG!"... Immediately, a head popped above the partitions right by where I knew the cash box was located. It was the private security guard. Mystery solved.

More Sheriff's deputies arrived and took the security guard aside to get his story. He claimed as he was doing his rounds, he found an unlocked door and thought he heard somebody inside, and went in to investigate. Except that he had no instructions to go inside, ever. Just patrol the outside. While they were grilling him, I took some other deputies in to where we had the video recorder and a monitor set up, to take a look at the footage. We saw him enter the room, walk directly to the center of the maze where the cash box is, then duck his head below the partition. At that point, the silent alarm was triggered, I made the 911 call; and in less than 3 minutes, the deputy, the dog and I enter.

Turns out the security guard had a record (burglary), and when he let them search his apartment, he had a lot of Powell products; T-shirts, sweatpants, etc. that would have been easy to remove from the warehouse in the times he had entered. He was not a skater, and could not explain how he got all this stuff. They also cited him with some illegal martial arts gear. There was no trial since he copped a plea when it was clear they had the goods on him.

After they took him away in a patrol car, and the original deputy came to me and said, “You know this maze of desks and partitions is perfect. How about the company letting us use it for training our police dogs.” I checked it out with George the next day, and it was agreed.

This was before the half-built SkateZone was open to the “public,” and one Saturday, all these patrol cars and police dogs showed up in front of the Lemon House. That’s why I have all these pictures of German Shepherds lounging around the SkateZone. That’s where they hung out while one dog at a time was next door in the hall of cubicles, training to play “bad-guy-in-the-maze,” their favorite game.

When you love your work, you get really good at it.

Chapter 19 The Taj Mah Wall

All along, the company had been moving our different departments and functions into the building right on the heels of the construction work. As each bay was completed and signed off for occupancy, Facilities would truck the production machinery and workstations out from Gutierrez Street.

The bays that were to become the indoor SkateZone were a low priority, having little to do with production and making a buck. Our ramp-building posse got together when we could to build a few improvements for the Parking Lot SkateZone, always keeping in mind how they would fit into the new space. Finally one day, the inspections were all completed, occupancy granted and the SkateZone could move inside.

I don't have a clear recollection of who was in charge of designing the SkateZone. George Powell approved the big picture, and Chris Iverson brought down George's decisions. I don't recall ever having any disagreement about the design and construction of any of that stuff. It must have been Iverson who had the call ultimately, but all designs seemed to come together by consensus. JW had the edge in design since not only had he studied all the parks on the West Coast, taking notes and making sketches, and he had skated all these elements to judge them in a way only a skater could. He could make drawings to communicate what he had in mind in a way that another skater could recognize as something he would want to skate. JW got his first paycheck from Powell Corporation for his SkateZone drawings.

The team for building all this stuff was composed of skaters that worked for the company like Ves, Chris, and Jamie, who and donated our time to be a part of it and most of Team Effigy: Mike Taylor, Robbie Olhiser, Mike Kresky, Jeff Pixley and JB Baxter; plus JW and me, and a character named Scott Graham who went on to build his own skatezone in Arkansas. In the whole process I didn't design any part; I just consulted on to how to build what the brain trust of skaters had come up with, though I think I had some part in instigating the Taj Mah Wall. It was a re-creation of something we had seen in one of Moose's skateboard videos. Some contest in a beach town south of LA where there was a giant quarterpipe set up at the bottom of a steep street where the skaters had an easy way to build up their speed. It was an easy sell. It was the first major permanent feature in the SkateZone. The rest of the ramps had been recycled from the parking lot configurations. As the biggest element we had built so far, the Taj Mah Wall would be too big to move. It dominated one end of the first bay, floor to ceiling, like half of a vert ramp.

By this time Jamie Johnston had become Chris Iverson's assistant in R&D and was becoming a key player in the SkateZone rampbuilding.

In our travels and our examination of these wood-framed ramps, it would be hard to miss the most characteristic failure and figure out what to do about it. A soft spot would appear after the ramp was in use for a while. Looking underneath you'd find that the 2" x 4" joist in that spot had split along the grain where it was end-nailed or screwed. Well, you could jack it back up into place and then screw a block of wood to the bulkhead to hold it. But if the soft spot were too close to the ground, you'd just have to jam some blocks under it. We came up with the idea to pre-empt that kind of failure by putting a little 2" x 2" piece of scrap plywood under each joist as a mini-ledger. We dabbed the block generously in a puddle of Titebond carpenter's glue and screwed it in place. With the glue block there, the split in the joist never gets started. By the time we got to working on the Taj Mah Wall, glue blocks were our standard procedure.

When you cut the bulkheads for the transitions, naturally you figure out how to get two bulkheads out of one sheet of plywood. Your leftovers turn out to be football shaped, and happily, the convex match for the same radius you're cutting the concave transitions. This is a big help when you go to bend the 3/8" plywood sheeting into place for screwing to the joists. Different strategies were employed to wet the plywood first, to help soften up the wood fibers without saturating them. Even so, trying to press the curve into plywood by standing on it, you were likely to have it break. But if you pushed on it with a curved press, the bending would happen over a larger area and not be concentrated enough to crack it at one line. With the football shaped left overs we rigged up something that looked to us like a rickshaw because of the long 2" x 4" extensions we used to brace it in place while we climbed on it to do the bending.

The second big feature we made for the indoor of course was a roll-in ramp with a crow's nest at the other end of the room to build up initial speed for a run at the pyramid or the funbox in the center of the room, or the banks and wall rides on the south wall, or the Taj Mah Wall.

In the early days of the SkateZone we had to maintain an official scenario that what we were creating there was that was not a public skatepark but a training facility for our amateur and professional team riders, which it was. Training for what? Training to have more fun! Its second official function was that it was R&D's testing ground for company products, which it was. The third function was to be our laboratory of the arts of skatepark design and construction, which it definitely was. With these guidelines mollifying Powell's liability insurer, we could go on doing our thing. More and more categories of skaters were included: pros from other companies, amateurs from other companies, employees of Powell, family of Powell employees, ramp building volunteers; the list got looser and looser. Finally a membership plan was formulated along the lines of Kevin Harris' system, and even that system got increasing looser.

It turns out, that little of that posturing is really necessary. Skateboarders are not the type to blame somebody else for their injuries. In fact I don't think you can find an example of a skateboarder's lawsuit; these people know the risks they are taking and own that.

Skaters exist in a complex and chaotic arena with no prescribed pattern or rules. Even so, there are surprisingly few times when they run into each other. Like ants in a frenetic anthill, they sort out potential crossing paths with a heightened sense of being able to assess the trajectories of others.

You could walk across that busy skatepark, the whole 120 feet with your eyes closed, and never have a skater collide with you. I've tried this. In fact it would probably be safer with your eyes closed. Most skater/pedestrian collisions result from a pedestrian trying to get out of the way. The skater likely has more control than the walker imagines, and the best he can do is to keep walking at a steady pace.

Chapter 20 Captain Safety

Besides the skatepark elements, there had been some fun stuff to build for the trade shows. One was an elaborate mockup of gas station; walls covered with old hubcaps, a pump island with vintage gas pumps and oil can racks, a big red canopy, with the triple-P Powell-Peralta logo spinning slowly on top. The theme was "Super Service," and all our sales reps in the booth were dressed as gas station attendants.

In addition to those corny trade shows, Facilities sometimes made props for the videos. For the 1989 video, "Ban This," our creations took me back to my own homemade skate scooter when I was 10 years old. They were well-made versions of the peach-box-on-a 2" x 4" scooter, except instead of two halves of a clamp-on roller skate from the 1940's, in the late 1980's, we had Independent trucks, Powell-Peralta urethane wheels, Bones Swiss ball bearings: the Mercedes-Benz of the Peach Box Scooters. They weren't gray this time, but olive drab army green, matching the theme of a recent trade show. We called them Armored Personnel Scooters.

As time went on, my duties were expanded into more mundane, less fun factory management tasks, and I had less time to be involved with the SkateZone building. I was put in charge of fire prevention, hazardous materials and a company-wide safety program. That kind of made me the in-house building inspector: the Sheriff of PCHQ. I took to wearing my gold “steal-your-face” skull with lightning bolt Grateful Dead tie tack on my shirt like a badge. When the fire department assigned us our own fire marshal to oversee our compliance factory wide, turned out he was a Deadhead too. We got along famously, but he never cut us any slack, and I never asked him to. He would give me a heads up if I were missing something, like if he spotted a cheaper or easier way of accomplishing a result. We teamed up to make the plant a tight ship.

One of the things I had to do was compile an archive of Material Safety Data Sheets, MSDS. There has to be on file an MSDS for every chemical or material in use in the entire factory, so if someone swallows it, or breathes its fumes, or it catches fire, we can look up what’s in it right now. I had to call or write to manufacturers to chase down the required paperwork, and keep it all in a big binder. MSDS was a system that had just come into being in the mid 1980’s for manufacturers, and some companies were unaware of the OSHA regulations. At one company, skeptical people I spoke to on the phone kept transferring me up their chain until I reached the CEO in a meeting with some of his managers. They put me on the speakerphone and grilled me about this so-called MSDS thing, and why I needed to know what was in their product. They thought I was a competitor trying to steal their trade secrets.

I took a night course in Hazardous Materials Handling at the nearby UCSB extension, so that I could have full knowledge of our situation and how our company fit into the required regulatory system. Others taking the course were a number of employees of Chevron Oil's local operations. Chevron at the time was running TV ads portraying the company as a protector of the environment. A blue butterfly fluttered over a seaside sand dune. A chain-linked fence had been erected to separate 2 acres of dunes from the 1000-acre El Segundo refinery, site of many, many leaks, spills and explosions, polluting the air and the groundwater since 1911. A voiceover asks, "Do people really go out of their way so a tenth of a gram of beauty can survive?" The fuzzy, warm feel-good voice answers itself, "People do," proclaiming themselves saviors of the endangered "El Segundo Blue."

The Chevron employees were pretty funny whenever the topic under discussion somehow produced a straight line. Sometimes by accident and sometimes on purpose, the instructor would phrase the current topic in a rhetorical question. "Do some toxic waste producers cut corners and cheat on disposal regulations to save money?" The Chevron managers would chant their punch line in unison, "People do," and cackled cynically.

Then there was the mandatory company safety program. Companies with even a few employees are required to have an active program to keep the workplace safe and the workers safety conscious. In the construction world, every small contractor is supposed to gather his crew periodically for a "tailgate meeting" to discuss safety matters, but they often don't bother.

Whenever it turned out that I was asked to conduct a safety meeting, my idea was to bring everybody into the awareness that "shit happens" by going around the group and telling our goriest construction accident stories. It's amazing how many people get shot with pneumatic nail guns, often in the head. Those things can be set to "bump fire," so that if you continuously hold the trigger down, it will fire a nail when you bump the tip against the wood and you can go faster. So if you're coming down the ladder with the trigger still pulled after nailing off some framing, your buddy is standing there holding the ladder and you're both looking the other way, BANG! He's got his hard hat nailed to his skull. I have shot one of those framing nails into my finger, cut another fingertip with a Skilsaw, fallen from high places, but I still have all my parts. Some of the craftsmen I admired most had shortened fingers due to a momentary misjudgment in the use of power tools. One moment, ZIP! and your fingertip is gone forever. No putting it back on, it was turned to hamburger. If those kind of stories give you the willies, that's the goal. Once everyone had gotten the willies, the safety meeting had served its purpose. Moving on.

In the PCHQ setting, that kind of safety meeting was appropriate for the production workers in their environment of powered machinery, but the office staff and cubicle workers have different hazards. The most common office accident is the bottom drawer of a filing cabinet is left open. Who knew? The drawer is left open and someone carrying a piece of paper or something doesn't see and trips over it.

We learned a lot about Ves' past when we took that Noodles tour to Nor Cal. After we left Derby Park in Santa Cruz, he guided us up the Loma Prieta Ridge, a small, forested mountain range running up the peninsula toward San Francisco. He had been a firefighter and driver for Cal Fire in this area, and had stories to tell about driving their equipment through impossible terrain. After that he had worked as an ambulance driver until he couldn't take it anymore. Responding to traffic accidents, he said, you get used to the gore, and the physical pain you're witnessing, and even the death; you have your training for that and you do your job. The thing that weighed the heaviest on ambulance drivers is the grief of the survivors. Ordinary people had been driving along on an ordinary day, when, BLAM! Suddenly their companion, or their parent, or child, or spouse, is dead. That's the hardest pain to witness. Or to do anything about.

Anyway, Ves had extensive paramedic and fire safety training, and was enthusiastic about helping out with our program. One of the requirements of standard safety compliance is putting up posters around the workplace emphasizing safety awareness in some way. Ves was always looking for ways to make everything more fun and lighten my load, so he created a series of comic safety awareness posters around the plant with himself posing in hardhat, reflective vest and fire extinguisher as “Captain Safety,” on the lookout for hazards. The class clown of Facilities.

Probably the most useful part of the safety program was the first aid training. After “shit happens”, comes, “What do you do about it?” The American Red Cross provides first aid training as part of their basic mission, and if you gather together enough students and a room to meet, they will set up courses and provide instructors, literature, props and CPR dummies. The training was open to anyone interested, and my goal was to have at least two workers from each department learn the time tested methods of stopping the bleeding, restoring the breathing and dealing with heat stroke, heat exhaustion and shock. Later on, when the SkateZone was up and running, those who had jobs in the park were required to have taken the first aid course, with emphasis on broken bones and concussions. It came in handy.

Now here’s the strange thing about skateparks. Take the way it is now. Outdoor concrete skate-at-your-own-risk skateparks are everywhere. The municipality posts some rules about having to wear helmets and pads, and park hours; but pointedly, there is nobody there to enforce them. Unlike a swimming pool, there is no lifeguard; if there were, anytime someone was injured with no pads, the municipality would be liable. Unsupervised, it is the skater’s own responsibility to follow the rules…or not.

The SkateZone existed before this enlightened age and to protect the company from liability, the park was not billed as a retail recreational business, but first as a training facility for our professional team and aspiring amateurs. Expanding on that idea, SkateZone became a private club. Membership was organized into a database, and each skater was given a picture ID, like the ones we saw being made at Kevin Harris' Skate Ranches in Vancouver. If skaters were under 18, they had to provide a notarized permission slip and liability waiver from their parents. In their individual files there were the names and numbers of who to call in case of emergency. At the entrance to the park, ID's were checked. In this format, the Company did take responsibility and therefore had to enforce the helmet and pad rules. There were many, many exceptions.

Of course there were injuries, mostly twisted and sprained ankles, and broken bones, but in each case, the staff smoothly did the first aid, made the calls, and transported the skater to the ER at Goleta Valley Hospital.

Chapter 21 The Deming Prize

So I found myself in my mid forties and working in a big factory, and I was even becoming part of management. I never would have imagined sitting on a surfboard at Pohoiki, that my mainland adventure would land me in a big gray manufacturing plant and that I would be digging it. I became intrigued with the problem solving presented by these repetitive tasks, like inventing a plywood pitman arm to replace the rope and pulley system they had been using to counterbalance the weight of the silkscreen printing the deck logos. There were always ways to improve on the way things were being done.

This is about the time military powers were blundering their way to the First Gulf War in 1990. I had been a draft evading political science major at UCSB during the Vietnam War and I learned there's always blindness, miscalculations and misrepresentations leading up to these catastrophes. I was watching with great interest since this would likely be the war of JW's generation, and I wanted to know, specifically, how it was all coming down.

Since I was likely to be out on my rounds locking up the plant at 5:30 p.m. when the ABC nightly news came on, I set my VCR to capture the broadcast every day. One night at the end of the broadcast there was a feature about Ed Deming. Who would have thought that a number cruncher would have anything to inspire me?

Deming worked as a statistician for different departments of the US government up until the end of WWII. He had developed his insights about quality control and how the American manufacturers could up their game enormously by paying attention to a few core principles. His ideas fell on deaf ears.

The War had devastated all of the manufacturing capacity of the industrialized world, except for North America. The factories of Europe and Japan had been reduced to rubble. America had vast natural resources, big steel mills and all the factories that had been building the Jeeps, tanks, airplanes, ships and bombs for the war were quickly converted to making consumer goods like cars and refrigerators. In that early post war period, US manufacturers could sell whatever they produced to a world that had no capacity to meet its own needs. Business was booming for domestic manufacturing and plant managers naturally congratulated themselves as geniuses. They didn't need Deming to tell them how to do things better.

I got my driver's license in 1960. By the time I was twenty-five, ten years later, I had owned a 1941 Ford woodie, a 1948 Dodge, a 1948 BSA motorcycle, a 1949 Oldsmobile, a 1954 Chevrolet, a 1954 Hillman, a 1957 Ford, three VW panel vans 1954-58, a 1958 Fiat and a 1962 Jaguar. I identify the year and make of all

American cars built from 1950 to 1961 at a glance. I could go to Cuba and perform tune-ups on their vintage cars with a screwdriver and crescent wrench by ear; those cars are like old friends.

I could never afford a car that was less than ten years old. By 50,000 miles, these cars were wearing out and guys like me trying to keep a used car running were constantly replacing peripheral parts and expecting the decline in the innards of the engine to reach the point that it would be major rebuilding or the wrecking yard. First it was a fan belt, then a radiator cap or radiator hose or radiator, then a water pump, then a battery cable, then a generator, then the points needed to be replaced, or the coil or the distributor, or spark plug wires, or the carburetor needed to be rebuilt. If you were a little more into it, you could do a valve adjustment, head gasket replacement, or a complete valve job or camshaft replacement. King pins, wheel bearings, u joints, clutch and pressure plates, throw out bearings, mufflers, and gaskets of all kinds might need replacement. As time went on, the engines began to burn oil more and more as the piston rings and rod bearings wore out. If you weren't up to doing major surgery, it was game over. At 100,000 miles you couldn't expect much more.

The point being that I've seen the component parts wear out with normal use again and again and I have put the wrench to many a bolt and nut on post war vehicles from the US and Europe. I can feel the softness of the steel.

Nowadays I drive Toyota Tundras. I have a 2001 and a 2005. I liked the 2001 so much that I bought a 2005 just like it so I would have another when the first one wore out. That was about three years ago. The 2001 will not wear out. At 285,000 miles, I've only replaced the belts, the battery and just now, the alternator. All the rest of that stuff has never worn out, and whenever I do put a wrench to anything on that truck, the hardness and the durability of the alloy is obvious. That's how much the quality of our vehicles has changed since I was a teenager: more than tripling their functional lifetime. W. Edwards Deming had a lot to do with that.

At the end of WWII, the US Army occupied Japan and took over all its governance. In an effort to stand the country on its own feet again General MacArthur's administration undertook rebuilding its former manufacturing capacity, restructuring it toward consumer goods. Ed Deming was part of the US team to guide a new manufacturing process from the ground up. Japanese industrialists took him very seriously.

In the early 1950's "Made in Japan" was synonymous with cheap junk. Manufactured goods were being made with accidental scrap metal alloys, "pot metal" we called it; whatever they could melt down and cast into something. They were clearly of lower quality than American goods and we scoffed at their pathetic knock offs of our products. By the late 1960's though, the Sony Trinitron had become recognized as the highest quality TV on the market. First Japanese made consumer electronics, and then all kinds of exports to the American market that were beginning to outclass everything made in the USA.

In 1974, we moved to Hawaii for the first time, and there was about half American made and half Japanese made cars and trucks on the island. Out in the rugged Puna district where many roads were just a swath of bulldozer scraped lava flows, we put our trucks through daily torture tests. Over the next 12 years, my pickups were a Chevy, 4 Fords, a Jeep and finally a Datsun. I ran them all into the ground until they were beyond repair. I used to caution my friends to never buy a truck from me as I likely had gotten every last bit of usefulness out of it. It became clear in this environment, that the Japanese trucks, especially the Toyota 4 X 4 pickups, would outlast them all. How did that all happen?

By 1980, Japan's reputation for quality products was unmistakable. In 1981 Ford Motor Company began having some of the automatic transmissions for its economy Ford Escort built in Japan by Mazda. American consumers soon became aware that the Japan-made transmissions were noticeably superior. The ones made in Ohio were erratic, shifted poorly through the gears and were generating drivers' complaints. Ford took notice and dismantled a number of the Mazda transmissions to figure out why. They discovered that while the Japanese tranny used the exact same Ford design as the American, Mazda was holding specifications to tighter tolerances, by a lot.

The specs for parts on complicated gizmos like automatic transmissions are written as a measurement "plus or minus"–an allowable deviation from the exact ideal number. The Japanese plant was somehow narrowing that sloppiness to the point where there was virtually no deviation, and the result was magic. At first it was thought that the Japanese had come up with technologically advanced machinery that was making the difference. Closer inspection revealed that the qualitative edge was the mindset of the teams along the assembly line. Deming's mindset.

Statistics always seemed to me like an inhumane discipline of cold mechanical calculations and heartless judgments, so I was surprised to find Deming's philosophy just the opposite. Here are the parts of his system that resonated with me. First was the idea to eliminate the barriers between departments and levels of management to the point where the whole group can operate as a single team, and then go a couple of steps farther to include the suppliers and the customer.

The Deming way is a commitment to constantly improving. Whatever it is you're making can be improved upon. The precision of the Mazda Ford Escort transmission was the result of a manufacturing culture in which the intelligence of every worker is tasked with improving quality. In the West, factories were run from the top down. The executives and the managers figured they had all the answers and workers would do what they were told, and quality control inspectors decided whether the results were good enough, or not. All departments were pushed to achieve numerical levels of production and the source of materials needed for production was the cheapest supplier at the moment. Post war manufacturing quality was just "good enough."

The Ford engineers who took a tour of the Mazda plant were surprised that there were no quality control inspectors and no bins of rejected parts to be sent back for repair, as there would have been at a Ford plant. Workers were encouraged to work at a pace where they could make a perfect part every time. There was no element of the fear of not keeping up with a prescribed pace since that pressure leads to error. Where there was an area that needed improvement, the approach was to provide the workforce with better materials, better tools, better procedures and better training. In fact, that's one of the ways a Deming statistician reads what's going on. If a number of production workers are doing the same repetitive task and there is a wide spread between their output, that is a flag that means very clearly there are gains to be made in the tools, techniques, ergonomics and procedures of that situation. In Deming's world, the data and the statistics of the production line are not used to judge the worker. They are used to make observations about the system.

In the old model, the managers figure out everything and the production workers do what they're told. "You're not paid to think!" Deming's system makes use of each worker's brainpower, and his acute awareness of how to improve that small part of the manufacturing process that's in his hands and in front of his eyes, and the nature of his own physical stresses. Make your processes less painful to the production worker, and errors go down, and your quality goes up, not to mention that that worker doesn't have to suffer to do the job that's been created for him.

I was able to make some small gains when my Facilities duties came in contact with the production line, but a management revolution would be required to make a big difference at Powell. But I was able to apply what I learned from Deming in everything I did and encouraged anybody I was working with to dial in the precision of whatever we were doing. We had built the Taj Mah Wall with that increasing concern for making the component parts identical.

We can all sense the superior quality of cars and trucks from Japan with which US automakers still haven't caught up. It's a matter that country is very proud of. How do the Japanese explain what happened? In Japan, the highest award for excellence in manufacturing is named "The Deming Prize," to honor the profound effect his guidance had in bringing the country's industrial base up from the ashes and rubble of WWII to become a high tech model for the world. The seminal technology of that revolution was Edwards Deming's human software of ideas.

Chapter 22 The Spine and Bowl

Back in Hawaii, that sweet little surf spot at Honoli'i Stream was the perfect place for JW to learn to surf. A very short paddle out took you to an easy shore break in shallow water. Just outside of that where the bottom dropped off was a generally larger shorebreak with lefts and rights. On the other side of the river mouth to the north and farther out was a pretty consistent left that could get big and tubular. If you were to design a surfing park that would be a treat for all levels of surf skills, this would be it.

A good skatepark is just like that; it has elements that provide fun for all skillsets, and incrementally more challenging banks and ramps to advance what you can do.

The largest element of the SkateZone was the spine ramp. A spine ramp is two halfpipes joined at their coping. It lets you drop in on one halfpipe, up and over the double coping of the spine and into the other halfpipe, like the ramp in Animal Chin. All the time the team was building out the first bay of the SkateZone, the question was whether George would allow the park to expand into the large bay next to the flatland side of the Zone, doubling the floor space of the playground. Once conceived of, the basic spine ramp pretty much designed itself given the limitations of the space.

The building was constructed of multiple bays of high arched barrel vaulted roofs. At the base of the arches, 10 feet off the floor, big steel tie rods stretched across the room, every 16 feet. Two bays were for the SkateZone. One bay we had filled with the flatland skate elements and the Taj Mah Wall. The second bay was for the spine and bowl.

To have maximum headroom at the rollouts and the spine, we needed the tie rods to be over the flatbottom areas. The ramp itself was 48 feet wide and the spine had three sections: a 36 foot spine with the double coping side by side, an 8 foot truncated spine with the two copings a foot apart, and a 4 foot wide rollover at the end, to provide options for various skill level. The rollout had different heights and in a nod to the beginnings of vert skating, one section had actual cast concrete pool coping in place of the steel pipe coping.

It just so happened my communal sister, Carol Latvala, was down visiting her son starting at UCSB and was there the night we opened the spine ramp for its first big skate jam. Members of the Bones Brigade were in town and we were going to have them have the honor of the first ride, but they were late in showing up, so we unceremoniously took down the caution tape and let everybody rip it up.

The last element we got to was the bowl. It had been in the works since the conception of the spine ramp. There was a large offset in the walls at the back of one halfpipe that would allow us a generous sized rectangular bowl. We set it up so that a second spine formed one edge of the bowl. Eventually a skater would be able to drop in on the first halfpipe, over the spine to the second halfpipe, and over another spine into the bowl. In the meantime, we built a temporary rollout that hovered over the unfinished bowl.

There wasn't any big push at that time to get the bowl completed. The rest of the SkateZone was up and running, and most of the crew that did the ramp building, including myself, had returned to our regular duties in the company. The first part of construction was easy; it was two intersecting halfpipes built with our standard methods. One went over vert up the concrete wall. Then came the tricky part; making the bowl corners.

It turned out the bowl corners became an act of one-man performance art. Jamie Johnston had the creative chops and most importantly, the patience to do the corners. It took a few months since his first priority was his work with Chris in R&D, whenever he could get an hour or two; he was in the bowl and focused. From my examination of Tony's bowl corners and advice from Frank Hawk, along with experiencing cutting compound angles for hip roofs, I could give Jamie some pretty good conceptual guidance, but he had to work out the details himself. At each level, the compound cuts would have to change both angles. He worked it out and single-handedly executed those bowl corners. Beautiful job.

Finally, there was the SkateZone in all its glory, and for the next three years it served the Jones of a whole generation of skaters. JW and the crew that were running the park continued to make additions to the street skating side of the park and many modifications to the Taj Mah Wall, including a place where you could climb up and drop in from the top, adding one more feature to up your skills.

Chapter 23 Jana, The Hap-Hap and The Dalai Lama

I'm not superstitious...but. When you have lived and worked on the quaking and steaming overgrown lava flows of East Hawaii and witnessed ten years of eruptions, you learn to have a sense of what Madame Pele wants...and what she doesn't want; what's Kapu. She has many potent ways to express herself, and the times and places she acts up are way beyond coincidental.

I grew up in Carpinteria and roamed around the beaches and hills all up and down the Santa Barbara coast. We had our supposed haunted houses, our corny made-up Indian legends, and ghost stories, but I never took that stuff seriously. I didn't have the idea that supernatural beings were part of my environment. I'll get back to that.

About the time the SkateZone was in full swing, I had a visit from an old girlfriend, Jana, from our commune days in San Francisco. She had been JW's nanny there from the time he was a few months old until he was two, 1971-73. We had last been together in 1980 when she came to stay with me in Hawaii for about ten really magic days. That was the closest I had come to having a committed girlfriend since I had broken up with JW's Mom, Patti, five years earlier. The thing is that besides being a fine artist, a beautiful and joyful companion, Jana is psychic.

She had timed her trip down from her home in Pacific Grove near Monterey, to coincide with the appearance of the Dalai Lama at UCSB, and a perfect time to catch up with me. This was Sunday, April 7, 1991, I still have the ticket stub. Having been somewhat of a Buddhist scholar when I went to college there, and a fan, I was eager to see him too. The talk was held in the packed UCSB Event Center. The acoustics were horrible. From where we sat, I could hardly make out what he was saying. After struggling to hear for a few minutes, I gave up and just felt the warmth and humor of his intonations and let that elevate me. Luckily, a few days later, or maybe the following weekend, the local public radio broadcast his entire speech, in perfect clarity, and I was able to hear every word of it sitting there at home in the Lemon House. I've read lots of Buddhist texts and attended many lectures and presentations. Many of them can be complex, murky and baffling, some intentionally so. The Dalai Lama's offerings on the other hand, are simple homilies that boil down a human condition into a crystal insight:

"When you think everything is someone else's fault, you will suffer a lot". – Dalai Lama

This was Jana's first trip to Southern California, and I was showing her around the whole South Coast.

There are creeks large and small that trickle down from the hills and many have a rudimentary road following them. We had driven up through a lemon orchard into a canyon that I had been to seven or eight times over the previous thirty years of explorations. It was beautiful; the little stream sustained Sycamore and Bay trees and filled small ponds here and there. The road was going right along the wide, mostly dry creek to the East when Jana started exclaiming, "Oh...Oh.Stop! Stop right here!" There was a wide enough shoulder to get off the road. I stopped. She jumped out and scampered down into the creek bed, and turned upstream where it veered sharply away from the road. "This way, come on." We had only gone about fifty yards to where the creek came out from under the grove of trees, and there we saw, obviously, what she had picked up on with her amazing sensitivity.

Rising up hundreds of feet from the east side of the creek was an enormous slab of sandstone tilted back from the vertical, a common formation in the Santa Ynez Mountains that form the ridge behind Santa Barbara. This particular bare monolith had a series of plainly visible shallow oval caves that followed a line angling up from the creek, getting progressively smaller. The indigenous Chumash who found such a site in their natural world, would have placed great significance on it. The village that had existed along that creek had been well documented as an important crossroads, but its native population been wiped out by the European diseases and the cruel subjugation of the Spanish intrusion. We had probably been riding up through a ghost town of that village, now overgrown and invisible as the natural materials that they built their shelters and sweat lodges with melted back into the landscape.

Some of the larger niches were big enough for two people to climb into, so naturally we climbed in, and being lovers at the time, we did some smooching and horsing around in there. Who knows what purpose the caves played in their culture. They could have been like thrones, or box seats for the chieftains or shamans to overlook a ceremony or gathering below on the wide gravel bank. Maybe this clearing was their church and the caves were like altars where they would place offerings. Maybe it played a part in the preparation of their dead. Whatever it was, it was likely that our foolishness would be Kapu to the ancient ones.

After about 20 minutes of enjoying this special place we retraced our steps back to the truck. I found a place to turn around after the creek had crossed the road. It was a warm day and we had the windows of the truck down. After a quarter of a mile, I noticed that there was a little whirlwind in the road that seemed to be following after us, and picking up speed. As the road came down into the lemons and straightened out parallel to the tree rows, the dust devil veered off into orchard on our left. The road continued another 75 yards straight and took a sharp left turn along somebody's property line. I could see the column of dust rising off in the lemon trees, and we were on a collision course. When we got to the tree row it was following, it came roaring out stronger than ever and seemed to go right through our open windows, filling the cab with a swirling mix of dust and pebbles and leaves, before it ran off and upward into the sky down toward the ocean.

I later learned that to the Chumash this kind of thing was well known. A dust devil was considered a Hap-Hap, an energetic spirit being that always appears with something angry to say.

Jana had never been in this part of the world, and didn't know anything about Chumash lore, but she found that place like there were searchlights attached to it. Magic things like that happen around her, like our time in Hawaii. That day, I'm pretty sure we were scolded by a genuine Hap-Hap for our irreverence in a sacred place.

Chapter 24 Escape From Planet of the Skates

I had been backloading my escape plan for quite some time. The Noodles Tours came to an end since the SkateZone had become an extreme skateboarding destination it made little sense to go anywhere else. Chris was spending more and more time with Jeannie and JW had his own car, so I didn't need Midnight for skate safaris anymore.

I bought a Jeep pickup with four-wheel drive and installed a mobile phone, in 1992, an early adopter. Mechanically, the Jeep turned out to be problematic. I hadn't quite learned my lesson about domestic vehicles, but it was the right size, I liked the look of it and I got a toolbox that I bolted into the bed.

The move to PCHQ turned out to be a miscalculation in the minds of many. It would be bizarre for me to criticize it, since everything worked to propel JW and me through the unfolding drama that would fulfill all our dreams. Nothing like the SkateZone would ever have happened. So I have to thank everybody that played a part in the way it all came out.

Once committed to this one big space, the company had lost its flexibility. It could grow but it could not shrink. Sales reached their historic peak about the same time we were moving into the building, and then plummeted when the skateboarding industry as a whole fell into one of its inexplicable crashes.

Something was going on at the core of the company. Powell-Peralta was the Santa Barbara group plus the L.A. group. In Santa Barbara, we made the products, with the exception of the videos. The L.A. group was the team and the video unit. It had always been a hyphenated company. When Stacy Peralta made a decision to back away from the company and pursue his career as a documentary filmmaker, it had an effect on morale at PCHQ.

For me the fun was going out of it anyway. With the industry undergoing one of its baffling cyclical downturns, new skateboard companies were starting up, adding to the competition in a diminishing market. Powell was especially hard hit, and the company had to scale back many of our dreams, and it was likely that the SkateZone would have to be dismantled, so that the space could be rented out as warehouse space or some other use, and there were going to be a number of layoffs in all departments. JW had moved down to an apartment near the City College, to begin to experience his freedom, and I was confronted with the fact that this stage of my parenting had come to an end, and it was time to be my own independent self again. I began to think, "Now where was I before I finally settled in to being a single parent and focused on taking JW on this adventure?" I felt drawn to the Bay Area where Dick and Carol had gone to work for the Grateful Dead. It was a well-known happy hunting ground, as far as building projects went.

Some of my favorite cohorts were gone from Powell. Joel Watson had moved on when he realized there was no future for him there. He had pushed a few too many buttons among management. I became the facility manager in his place, a role I could fill with success in most areas, but I wasn't a natural honcho like Joel had been. And I was experiencing the pressures and antagonisms of his position.

It all started out to build some ramps for my kid and take him on an adventure. Mission accomplished. So what was I still doing there? I wrote a haiku that summed up my state of mind at this time.

Summer morning.
Facility manager
Wears a hat full of bees.

If I hadn't resigned, I might have been laid off, or worse, someone else who really wanted or needed the job would have lost his job instead of me. I had lost my inspiration, especially since an upcoming "building" project would likely be the DE-construction of the SkateZone ramps. If there is anything I couldn't bring myself to do, it was the dismantling of that skatepark, or any skatepark. That would be the ultimate un-fun. Anti-fun. Especially since I had something to do with building it. I'd have been sick the whole time.

I was in this mood when it came time for my main

funnyman, Ves Fowler, to go. On the one-year anniversary of the horrific death of his son, he began to have reactions that would be described as "post traumatic stress" and could no longer trust himself to operate machinery, drive, or deal with the daily workings of the skateboard factory. We agreed that I should lay him off, for medical/psychological reasons. He had always been dependably fun. That was my last official act as facility manager, to lay him off. Then I laid myself off.

The hat full of bees was gone, and I was free again. I packed it all up and was out of there fast. Once I decided, there were wings on my feet. George Powell came out to say goodbye as I drove my last load of belongings off to storage. He wished me well and I him. I didn't see him again for twenty years when JW and I encountered him and Jim Fitzpatrick at the Santa Barbara Film Festival, attending a showing of the new film, Skatistan, about a group of European skaters setting up a school and skatepark in Kabul, Afghanistan.

Chapter 25 The Aftermath

JW and the gold pyramid moved back from his downtown apartment into the Lemon House, where he lived until the SkateZone was dismantled in 1994 and the Lemon House was torn down. They had a bunch more fun there, turning it into a bunkhouse for visiting skaters. Somebody else will have to tell that part.

JW began to find his own path and put his video skills to work. After SkateZone was closed, he started working with a small Santa Barbara skateshop called The Church of Skatan. He made two skate videos for them, and by the time he was through with that, he got hired as a cameraman for Powell's 1995 Bones Brigade Summer Tour and he traveled with the team across the US and Europe. Later that year he produced and edited the latest Powell video, Scenic Drive.

Myself, I headed back to the San Francisco Bay Area, the part of the world that feels most like home to me. About the time I was packing up to leave, in October 1991, there had been an enormous wind-driven firestorm, a "sundowner," that swept down from the Oakland Hills through tangle of narrow winding streets destroying 3450 homes and killing 25 people. It was a replay of the Painted Cave Fire above Santa Barbara that we had watched from the roof of PCHQ in

July 1990 that "only" took out 425 houses and killed 1 person.

The hills of Oakland and Berkeley face west toward the San Francisco Bay and nearly every single house there had a view of the Bay, Alcatraz Island, the San Francisco skyline and the Golden Gate Bridge. 12 years before I had learned my construction chops in these hills, first a year with Gary Cohen remodeling houses studying for my own contractor's license; then a year with Mark Taylor and his "Satori Japanese Bath Company." I built over 50 hot tubs in those hillsides.

I had always considered those hills to be a constant supply of projects. With such unbeatable views, owners couldn't get a better location, so the only way to improve one's living standard was to remodel. Now with 3450 houses suddenly gone, there would be endless work for somebody like me.

I moved up north and signed up with a temporary agency, connected with a few projects, and almost immediately ran into the very last girlfriend I had on the mainland 15 years before, Katie Flick. I was taking part in a remodeling project in Berkeley, and at lunch I would walk down to College Avenue for a burrito. She was running a little artisan jewelry store next to the burrito shop, and she saw me walking by. I wouldn't have recognized her, because now she had long straight red hair, when before she had short brown curly hair. She looked a lot different done up in a slinky dress, but I recognized her voice. She had been a whole lot of fun in 1978 and 79 when I worked for Gary and Mark. I had broken it off with her when I moved back to Hawaii to raise JW.

She was managing an apartment building in the nearby Rockridge District, and had a vacant studio right next to hers and I took it. At first, I had been alternately staying at motels or crashing at Dick's house, but now I had steady work and I was ready to have a place of my own, with a little kitchen, space for my stereo, VCR and TV, and a desk for my computer, and AutoCad set-up. There was a big window over my desk that looked right straight up at that great ashen swath of the burned area.

I think I was there for about 3 months. We had a whole bunch of laughs then, and we went to at least one Grateful Dead show at the Oakland Coliseum, but mainly she was toying with me and making her boyfriend jealous. He was the one she was focusing on now, and it gave her some satisfaction to have me chase her for a little while. It was fun anyway. About the time I figured that out, Dick called me up. He had been with his second wife for about four years, and they were breaking up. Did I want to be roommates with him? In short order, Katy let me out of my 6-month lease, and Dick and I got an apartment in Richmond. We stayed there for a few months until he was able to buy a house in Petaluma, across the bay and north up 101 in Sonoma County. It wasn't until I lived 30 miles away that I got a project in the burned area just uphill from my Rockridge studio window.

Meanwhile, back in the skateboard world, life went on. Jim Fitzpatrick had set himself on a mission about the time we came to work at Powell. He wanted to see the institutionalized obstacles of the liability laws and the culture of high stakes litigation give way to a day when skaters could simply skate at their own risk at local facilities in public parks like other pastimes; basketball, soccer, baseball.

With a role in Powell's promotions department, Fitz had relentlessly promoted a larger world for skateboarders. He was the emcee during the Summer Tour 1988. He was a leading force in the MacKenzie Park SkateZone, and all the parking lot and indoor SkateZone contests. Sometime after I departed the company, Fitz formed an industry association to lobby for changes in the liability laws. Finally, after countless meetings with bureaucrats and public officials, hearings before commissions and boards, and letter writing campaigns, sometime in the late 1990's, he was able to get skateboarding added to the list of "Hazardous Recreational Activities," HRA's; a legal designation of an inherently dangerous activity. Therefore, skaters skate at their own risk and are responsible for their own injuries. That's all it took; for the state government to officially recognize that skateboarding is dangerous. Duh.

With that out of the way, municipalities all over California could relax and allow these recreational zones to exist without perceived multi-million dollar risks. The idea of the extreme liability of skateboarding turned out to be bogus. Fitz had researched all the available data and found there were far fewer injuries in skateboarding than there were in many sports like baseball and swimming. The only deaths associated with skaters happened when they collided with cars. There are no cars in a skatepark. And interestingly, he discovered there had been no successful lawsuits against a skateboard park ever. Zero. Even trial lawyers would have to admit there was no cash cow to defend.

The Skatepark in Tijuana, North Vancouver Snake Bowl, Uplands Skatepark, Derby Park in Santa Cruz; those were the precursors of today's free outdoor concrete skateparks; a way to let the kids entertain themselves in their chosen sport. At last, in the year 2000, "Skateboarding Is Not a Crime." By 2017, outdoor concrete skateparks are everywhere. Fitz fought the law, and everybody won.

Chapter 26 The Digital SkateZone

Dick and Carol had shared homes and adventures with Patti and me in San Francisco and Hawaii, in the 1970's. JW and their son Rich were born about a year apart, when we were living communally.

Now years later both couples had broken up, and in 1993 Dick and I got a place in Petaluma. With a four-bedroom house, we each had a bedroom and another room. His second room was dedicated to the storage of his music tapes. Mine was my office. I had set it up with deluxe build-ins, a guest bed and a large desktop for the monitor, keyboard and digitizing pad that constituted my AutoCad studio. The garage became my woodshop, the best personal shop I ever had.

Dick had become the Grateful Dead tape archivist, and Carol worked in the Grateful Dead Ticket Office. In 1995, Carol was able to buy the house right next door to us, and in a way, our commune was revived. I took down the fence between the two backyards.

When his duties didn't take him down to the band's Front Street studio in San Rafael, the living room was Dick's workspace. His job, literally, was to listen to recordings of Grateful Dead concerts, and to find among the thousands of concerts, those most worthy of a CD release. By the time he was through, the band had released 14 shows, in a series named after him, "Dick's Picks."

The living room was simply furnished; couch, armchair, coffee table. At the end of the room toward the kitchen was a big black cabinet I had built for the sound gear; amps, tuner, cassette recorder, cd player behind black glass doors, and on top, a reel to reel tape deck, sometimes two. On another wall opposite the couch was a pair of high tech Meyer Sound powered studio monitors provided by the band, one on either side of the big TV.

Adjoining the living room was a tiny kitchen and a dining room. The gold pyramid from my days at Powell dominated the space. We set up a cat tree inside of it for Dick's cats, Leroy and Lucy.

Back to the point: between construction projects, with my computer drafting studio all set up, and with JW's encouragement, I finally found the time to construct the 3-D digital SkateZone in AutoCad.

I had drawn the floor plan years before, and I had taken precision measurements of everything, including all the elements: Taj Mah Wall, spine ramp and bowl, and even the ceiling, roof and tie rods. I just needed to advance my skills at drawing the curved surfaces of the ramps so I could make an exact wire frame model of the park. And that's what I did. This was done on AutoCad Release 10, which was a powerful program even then. I could view the park from any point in space; inside the park looking any direction, even from outside the park looking through the wire frame of the roof or walls. It took me over a month to get that far, and I was just learning how to put surfaces on the wire frame and how to construct visual fly-throughs when I ran out of time and money so I had to return to making a living. Necessity is the father of adventure and I soon connected with a new mission.

Chapter 27 The Great White Duck

The one project I had that had been part of that Oakland Hills firestorm was after I moved to Sonoma County. It had been a luxury home of a big time telephone company executive and it had burned completely to the ground. It had been at the very southeast corner of the fire on Grizzly Peak Blvd., at the top of the ridge. The house next door to the south was untouched, and the undeveloped natural landscape across the road had been slightly scorched.

Going around meeting the crew on my first day there, I discovered that one of the carpenters, Andrew Gordon, lived in Petaluma also. It turned out he lived about a half a block from me, and he had been to more Grateful Dead shows than anybody I ever knew. After that we commuted together for the rest of that project and many others.

The foreman on the Grizzly Peak house was Gary Crawford. He was the only person in my construction life that would get to the job earlier than I did. Andrew and I would pull up there a good half hour or more early every day and he'd already be there, standing by his truck in the dark smoking a cigarette. He had a good layer of blubber that insulated him so well that he wore short pants in any weather, but his weight never slowed him down. He was a relentless hard worker and equally relentlessly careful about what we were building. And of course he was funny. He kept running gags going and had a nickname for everybody. At first I was "Gun Turret John," for the weeks I had been doing the finish work from planks on a scaffold up in the turret-like skylights at the Grizzly Peak house. By the time we reached Coarsegold, a couple of projects later, I was "Johnny Be Good."

In 1994, Gary invited Andrew and me to build a house with him from the ground up. The site was near Coarsegold in the Sierra foothills about 25 miles south of Yosemite. Gary's approach to building was as if he had arrived at Deming's methods independently. It was an eye-opener to work with him closely building an entire house. Up until then we had done remodels and additions together. We began with a bare plot of ground in the woods adjoining a 5-acre lake, with no other houses within sight. There wasn't any electricity to the job yet and a couple of poles would need to be added to bring wires in from the road, so we built most of it on generator power.

The care with which Gary proceeded began with a solid set of batter boards and precisely located screws to tie the strings for our layout. A backhoe and operator were hired to make the foundation trenches, and to grade the site. Now, working with most builders, the concrete foundation walls that are below grade are of little concern. Gary had us keep the forms for the stem walls perfectly plumb all the way to the bottom of the trench. Most builders will say you don't need to do that as long as the level where the sill plates are bolted down is in the right place. Gary's idea was that when your start compromising and saying "good enough" at the bottom of the trench, by the time you get to the peak of the roof, it's going to add up to "not good enough." That's pure Deming thinking.

At first it was just Gary and I until we got to the point of building the forms and tying the steel. After that, Andrew drove up to join us. One day shortly after Andrew arrived Gary said he was going to buy us lunch, so we all got into one truck and drove down to a local burger joint. Gary went in first and stepped up to the counter to order, "Three cheeseburgers and two chocolate shakes." Andrew and I looked at each other wondering why only two drinks when Gary turned to us and asked, "And...what are you guys having?" His capacity to put away food was a continual amazement.

Once the concrete was poured and the forms were stripped, we set to work on the sill plates and floor joists, taking great care to keep the plates as straight as a string while bolting them down. The floor joists we cut to the precise measurement, even though most builders would be fine with plus or minus 1/16", Gary's concept was; "Why not cut it exactly right?" To start with, he introduced us to the idea of calibrating our tape measures.

We all have these steel tape measures and they have a way of becoming inaccurate through normal use. It's that hook on the end that can make trouble. All the inches on the tape stay exactly the same, but that first inch can lead you to an inaccuracy of 1/16" by itself, and since all measurements have that first inch, they are all off. Which wouldn't be too much of a problem if we were all using the same tape for the whole project. But that isn't the case; we all had our own tapes. That hook on the end of the tape slides in and out the thickness of the hook, so that if you butt the end of the tape into something it will slide in that tiny amount, and if you were going measure the length of something you could hook on the end, it would slide out that same amount to compensate. So what you do to calibrate the tape is to dial in that hook. It can get its little slot the rivets go through clogged with dirt, glue, caulking or plaster, and it won't slide right making your butted measurements not agree with the hooked ones. That seldom happens. What does happen often is that hook gets bent.

So what you do is get a board or workbench surface with a sharp edge and measure a perfect inch from the edge using any other part of the tape but that first inch. You use the sharpest pencil to make the thinnest line. Then you hook your tape on the edge and see what it reads. Most often if it's off it's because the hook has bent inward, so the reading will be a little short. You take your hammer and tap that hook until it reads just right. When you've got three or four carpenters working on the same structure, just the fact that their tape measures read slightly differently adds up to a certain amount of slop. In most builders' minds, it's good enough, but not for Deming, Gary Crawford, and now me.

Likewise most framers will use a thick flat carpenter's pencil to mark their cuts, and as it loses its sharpness, the line it's making gets fatter and fatter until it's more than 1/16". Then you've got to decide which side of the line your saw cut is going to be on. Again, with multiple individuals the collective result is slop, so we kept sharpening our pencils by stropping them on a flat piece of sandpaper.

On the little lake there were about seven mallards and one large white duck. We took to feeding them pieces of our donuts one morning break. After that whenever we shut down the generator for break or lunch the ducks would turn and swim toward our shore, the big white duck first with the mallards following. He was definitely their leader. He was the first to waddle up to where the donut pieces were landing, with the mallards cautiously coming up behind. If you threw a whitish piece of donut or bread they would rush to be the first to get it, but if you tossed a piece of a brownie they would turn and run away figuring that it was a rock. After we got power company electricity and stopped using the generator, Gary would make quacking sounds at break and lunch and Howard, one of the white duck's nicknames, would turn and swim to join us with his mallard entourage paddling along behind.

You could build an entire house measuring and marking each piece with a square and pencil, and cutting it with a skilsaw on a pair of sawhorses. There would be a lot of variation in the squareness of the end cuts and the lengths of nominally identical members. Factor in fatigue, discomfort, and tedium and the sloppiness compounds itself.

In a Deming analysis, it's not the carpenters' fault, though some would perform better than others. It's nobody's fault; it's a flag that the situation needs (1) better procedures and training; like calibrating tapes, sharpening pencils and adding a half second of sharpened awareness before pulling the trigger and making the cut. And/or the situation would benefit from (2) better tools: like when there are a lot of members that need to be the same length, like studs, or cripples and trimmers for windows that are the same size, you set up a chop saw table so that the cut ends square every time, and you can set up stop blocks to cut repeated lengths and a built-in tape on the fence so that no measuring and marking even needs to be done. And/or less variation might be achieved with (3) better materials.

So you get a big load of lumber delivered from a local supplier and you may have blown it already if you only considered the price. Framing lumber has irregularities. You do the best you can and still it isn't perfect. You take the stack of materials that are going to be the wall studs. In California, most suppliers will sell you precisely precut 92 1/4" studs, so that with the addition of a bottom plate and two top plates, the stud wall is 96"+ tall. You are going to need a lot of shorter cuts of that same material for cripples and trimmers, so you get more studs than you need so you can "upgrade your stock," as we call it. We set aside the best for the studs. The others; the ones with curves in them or big knots that will weaken them, or some "wayne" which means a place where one edge is bark; those we put aside to use as shorter pieces and braces. Sometimes you'll get a load of 2" x 10"s, for instance, of the different lengths your plan calls for, and for whatever reason, maybe they came from different mills, some of them were 9 1/4" wide and the others more like 9 3/8". That's going to be a problem if they are end to end in the same floor, for instance. We always have a planer on the job to make the framing members the same dimension...another way of upgrading your stock.

It made sense to rent a vacation house at nearby Bass Lake, rather than rent motel rooms. In the fall off-season the lake was drained, so rents went way down. We each had our own bedroom and we had a kitchen to make our meals and lunches. We began calling Gary "Housemother." When we started, it was the middle of the summer and we were working 12 hours a day in the sweltering heat. As time went on the days got shorter and the nights got cooler so by the end it was winter and it was so cold we were putting our hands on the blazing halogen work lights until our gloves started to smolder, then we could go back to work. A hard worker day and night, Gary spent most evenings going over the plans, doing material take-offs for the next lumber drop, and going over the details.

Framing a house is not rocket science. It's pretty simple, and before long we had built the subfloor and had all the stud walls standing on the top plates. At that point, most builders would just start putting the plywood sheathing on. Gary added a whole day's work to fine tune the skeletal building in a process he called "plumbing and lining." He'd start by having us use string to check the straightness of the top plates, adjusting them and holding them in place with temporary braces, and making sure the walls were exactly as long they were supposed to be. He had invented some Plexiglas jigs that would clamp over the double top plate and hold the string of a plumb bob exactly 1" away, and with 1" x 1" blocks we could quickly check the stud walls for plumb, adjust them and use long diagonal braces to keep them from racking back.

With all our care in using the straightest lumber for the studs, some of them would still bow in or bow out. You can take a long string attached to the screw on your batter board and pull it up across the outer plane of the stud wall to check which studs need correction. Gary had a few methods to straighten the studs in place by notching and pinching, or by notching and shimming. Every stud corrected was held in position by a brace to the floor. Rejected studs are fine for temporary braces.

Then we plumbed and lined the interior walls. With all the framed walls braced every which way, the inside of the building was a web of lumber, and the outside all in an uncluttered plane. When we put the 1/2" plywood sheathing on, it became obvious that all the care we had put into the fine tuning made this step come together with no adjusting, fudging, shimming or trimming. Edges of the 4' x 10' sheets land exactly on the center of the studs, and the surface becomes a perfect plane, with no bulges or dips. Once that is nailed off every 6" on the edges and 8" in the field, those walls are not going to rack, but you leave all the braces in place until they need to be removed. There's no hurry to take them down and for a few weeks, all that green lumber can dry while held in position. It wants to stay the way it has dried.

Well, I'm an ace when it comes to building hip roofs, and it was my pleasure to build the pyramidal roofs on the two wings of this house. With the perimeter of the top plate a dependable perfect square, everything fit together like the parts of a Mazda transmission.

The windows and doors went in with minimal adjustments of the rough openings, and then it was time for Andrew and I to go home. The rest of the project was done by Gary and the local subs he had rounded up: electricians, plumbers, sheetrockers, painters, cabinetmakers, roofers, and for the exterior, a stucco contractor. It was years before I returned there and took pictures of the finished project.

We had nicknames for Gary: "Mr. Large," or "Oh Large One," when addressing him directly, and

"Housemother," of course, but in the following years we spoke of him respectfully as "The Great White Duck."

Chapter 28 SkateStreet

It had seemed that my skateboard period was over in 1991, and it was, for about the next six years. JW had kept working at Powell, moved back into the Lemon House and was part of the crew that managed the SkateZone as a retail business until it was dismantled in 1994. JW began to make his way in the world as an action sports videographer, following the bliss he had found in his high school class; making skate movies.

Well, by 1997, he and our old buddy from Powell, Mike Taylor, had been contacted by people who wanted to build the ultimate indoor skatepark in Ventura, and wanted to hire JW and MT to design and build it for them. And to my great thrill, they asked me to help them pull it off. MT and JW would collaborate with the two young entrepreneurs/skaters on the overall design, and when they came to a specific conclusion about what, JW would draw sketches, confident I could figure out how to build it.

People who actually skate have to be the ones to make the call about where and how high and what radius the transitions should have. I was pretty hip about ramps but being a non-skating carpenter, I was just the enabler, the structural consultant.

I moved back to Southern California for the duration of the project. I needed a simple place to stay and I lucked out. Legendary snowboard maker Chuck Barfoot had his house in La Conchita, and in the front yard he had a little housetrailer that he rented out. Best landlord I ever had. I didn't need much, just a place to shower, sleep and set up my computer. I could open the door of my trailer and see the break at Rincon through binoculars. It was a surfer's dream location, except I didn't get in the water the whole time I was there. It was pretty much 12 hours a day, 7 days a week for me, coordinating the irregular schedules of the revolving crew at SkateStreet. I like it that way; obsessed with my own sport and wanting to be there for every turn of a screw.

This was an ideal confluence of factors. There was an adequate budget. It was being created by partners Tim Garrety and Roger Thompson, with Erik Payne their main hands-on guy, in conjunction with a Christian youth group. They had a backer who financed everything and worked with them on a vision of how the park might be self-sustaining: with retail space, a café on a mezzanine overlooking the skating, advertising space on the walls. The building had smooth concrete floor, high ceilings, few posts, and plenty of room. Construction was to be done by JW, Mike Taylor and myself, supervising Erik's revolving workers from the youth group and whatever friends JW, MT and I could round up; Robbie Olhiser, Mike Kresky, Jeff Pixley, Jay B, Shane, and even Doug Hechter and his son Jake.

My old pal Ves came back into my life. He had reinvented himself this time as a cowboy poet musician. He wore a big cowboy hat and had gotten pretty good on the guitar. We got him hired at Skatestreet.

Work on the retail spaces was handled by local contractors and I had nothing to do with that, except that I did come into contact with the building inspectors. They did a little head scratching about how the building code applied where things were not designed to be safe in the normal way. You can't have railings along every side of the platforms, for instance; you're supposed to go over the edge, on wheels no less. In the end they concluded that we were building "recreational equipment" and that it was none of their business. I think they had us extend the fire sprinklers under the vert ramp rollouts that we had enclosed for storage of the templates and tools, but that was it.

Tim and Roger wanted nothing but the most excellent skate facility anywhere, so somehow they found Mike and JW, and pushed them to pull out all the stops.

We got to scheming about how to take everything up a notch. We were going to have to cut curved bulkheads out of 3/4" plywood, lots of them, with all different radiuses. Typical in the rampbuilding world was to cut the transition bulkheads with a jigsaw, or even more crudely, a Skilsaw. This method leaves irregularities in the radiused edge that within limits are deemed good enough since there would be a surface of plywood and a layer of Masonite that would bridge the imperfections. This is where my Deming mindset found its highest application. I had become accustomed to using a big 1-½ HP router and pattern bits to cut large architectural elements in my projects up north. It was an easy choice in this circumstance. Following a template we would make those curved edges very smooth.

Ordinarily a ramp builder would find a way to draw an arc with a pencil and a long stick with a nail in it. He'd make and draw a pattern on a piece of Masonite or plywood and use that over and over to mark out his bulkheads. It always worked well enough, for most purposes, but we were tasked to go all out. The Santa Barbara Mill and Lumber was known to me to have a big CNC router setup. CNC means Computer Numerically Controlled. They can feed a 4' x 8' sheet of any material and cut out the parts of complicated woodworking projects – cabinets, furniture, whatever, and mass-produce identical parts. So the decision was made to have them do our very simple radius templates with a precision difficult to achieve by other means.

We could get a different radius cut into each side of a sheet of HDF particleboard. We called them our "dogbones" and treated them like precision instruments. We only used our dogbones to carefully make secondary router templates, and then stashed them back in the dogbone closet. With the hundreds of repetitious cuts to be made, the templates would get dinged many times and repaired with Bondo until they would need to be replaced, and we'd bring out the appropriate dogbone again.

Accomplished skaters have little problem skating on irregular surfaces. In the process of learning how, they've rolled over every kind of hard surface never meant to be skated on; streets, sidewalks, ditches and rubble, where a pebble or crack can send you tumbling. They've skated on ramps with a bump here or a soft spot there and learned how to compensate, but if they had their druthers, they would want it to be as close to perfect as possible.

The first major thing we were going to build was the full vert halfpipe. If there was anything we would want to be geometrically perfect, this was it. This would be the most high-performance, high-speed element in the building; where skaters pushing the limits of the possible would be able to depend on the ideal predictability and uniformity of the surface, and concentrate in their own moves.

The big vert ramp was going to need a lot of identical bulkheads of 3/4" plywood. After seeing the CNC dogbones being produced, we decided that, for this one ramp, with over 100 3/4" plywood bulkheads to be cut, we would have SBML do them perfectly. It saved us a lot of hard, tedious work; it saved us a lot of time; and gave us a good head start knocking out one of the major centerpieces.

The rest of the vert ramp's construction was pretty much standard. We began to use a pneumatic pin nailer to hold the glue block joist ledgers instead of screws, holding them in place until the glue dried. It was faster and you didn't have to fight the screw trying to rotate the block. Pneumatic staples would probably be even better.

One of the most challenging and unique elements of SkateStreet was the repurposing we did around the building's loading dock at the room's northeast corner. Its lower level was 20 feet wide to accommodate two trucks, side by side, through the big roll-up doors; and it sat 4 feet lower than the skatepark floor. We built a big quarter pipe, a la SkateZone's Taj Mah Wall, beside the pit so a skater could go up the wall, down into a halfpipe with no flatbottom that filled the loading dock, gain even more speed, and launch up and over an odd element reminiscent of a giant Darth Vader helmet. Altogether, you had to call it the "Taj Mah Hole."

The very first thing we built in that room was a rectangular platform in the far northwest corner, to be used as a stage for music groups, etc. Eventually we would incorporate it into the ramp topography to become a skateable bandstand. JW set up his drawing table there with a panoramic view of the room, and his camcorder to document the action. All the time, I was taking pictures, and JW was drawing pictures; and now he was making videos.

SkateStreet was meant to be a park for all ages and skill sets. A second shorter less intimidating halfpipe was planned, next to the taller vert ramp, and a separate protected beginners area of the park for the smallest skaters, with adjoining seating area for parents.

As we began to fill up the room with different banks, Mike and JW's grand strategy came into focus. The "parallelomid" was a six-sided irregular truncated pyramid in the middle of the floor. Each face was parallel to the face of the opposite ramp, bank or roll-in across the floor from it. Roll-ins came from the corner of the vert ramp that shot you down toward the parallelomid, which you could attack in any number of ways. One goal was to have it so that with the momentum of the first drop, a skater could make an entire circuit of the room, pumping on the transitions, and never pushing off with his foot.

A marvelous thing was happening while we were getting the skate elements built. As we finished each, Roger's Mom, Elain, began painting murals on the walls behind them. Behind the vert ramp, she painted a cityscape of tall buildings that gave you the impression that the ramp was on a rooftop among them. Facing that wall you were facing in the direction of the Los Angeles suburban center and its skyscrapers. Behind the smaller halfpipe she painted a snowscape with a snowboarding halfpipe that seemed to be an extension of the Masonite one. Looking up that snowy channel you were facing northeast toward the slopes of the

Sierras. On the north wall, snow covered mountains blended into the green hills of the Ventura skyline, the same as you would see in that direction outside. On the west wall, of course, the green hills came down to the ocean and our familiar coastline with the Channel Islands in the distance. Appearing to extend out into the ocean from the stage in the northwest corner where JW made his drawings was a depiction of the Ventura pier. The rest of the west wall was to be the backdrop for our final masterpiece. A long wall was to be an element that would appear to be a breaking wave, with a section of over vert, behind which Roger's Mom would paint...a breaking wave. I couldn't be prouder of anything I was ever a part of building. The whole room was a masterpiece of her murals.

The Wave Wall; there it was: A sunny day in Pohoiki; a stationary perfect wave in plywood, Masonite and steel. Mission accomplished.

By the time we had finished this skatepark, I felt that I had finally satisfied the dream of being part of something like the Animal Chin Ramp that I had felt was the ultimate back in 1987, only 11 years before. Down the rabbit hole and back.

JW enrolled in formal professional training in state of the art videography next door to SkateStreet at the Technology Development Center, taking those skills up a significant notch. In the following years there, working with those same SkateStreet guys, he created a surfing video, Follow the Leader; and three skateboarding videos highlighting skating at SkateStreet: Welcome to Paradise, Return to Paradise and Time Machine. By this time his artistic and computer tech skills converged into some astounding motion graphics.

I went back to Northern California, and moved in with Carol. That's where I am today, 20 years later, trying to write some of this down.

Chapter 29 The Gold Pyramid

In 1999, tragically and unexpectedly, my friend Dick Latvala had a heart attack, fell into a coma and died 10 days later. I was living in Carol's house next door. He had lots of friends in the music world that would visit him there in his living room in Petaluma over the years. Among them was Kirk West, the road manager for the Allman Brothers Band. He had met Dick during one of the ABB collaborations with the Grateful Dead. He would find time to come up to visit whenever his band played the Bay Area.

As it happened, the Allman Brothers were playing at Shoreline Amphitheater in the South Bay and Kirk was in town. He came rushing up to Petaluma when he discovered what was happening. In the living room, a hospital bed had replaced the couch and Dick was lying comatose. As with the many heart-wrenching scenes that took place that week, Kirk's grief flooded the room.

In a few hours, Kirk had to get back down to Shoreline, and was getting ready to leave. He had long admired the Gold Pyramid, and we promised to give it to him if we ever got tired of it. Now he wanted it to remind him of Dick. A few months later as the house was being readied for sale, I packed it up and sent it off to Macon, Georgia. Kirk lived in a Victorian that's part of the Allman Brothers history. Today, it's a museum for the band, the "Big House." That's where the Gold Pyramid ended up, I think, in Kirk West's backyard.

Carol is my best friend, housemate, best landlady I ever had, astrologer, and cohort in our comic lifestyles and bizarre adventures since 1970. She encourages each of us to tell the story that we alone can: the tale of our unique path through this plane, seen through the prism of our individual being.

That's what I'm trying to do here. It's hard because of how much I have to leave out. So I've narrowed down this telling to the thread of skateboarding. Then I have to figure out where to stop, because these adventures continue to this day. Coming soon is the thirtieth anniversary of The Animal Chin premiere May 7. 1987. That will bring the whole thing full circle once again.

Chapter 30 Uncle John's Web

Again, JW went his way and I went mine. My adventures were as fun for me as his were for him. I'll get to tell mine later, but right now I'll stick with the anti-gravity thread.

Before you knew it, JW was producing skateboarding segments for the Blue Torch TV series on Fox Sports channel. Among the seven segments he produced, was the grand opening of the Santa Barbara Skatepark on the beach at the foot of State Street, a culmination of the dreams and efforts of so many people we knew and who we played and worked with.

His video work expanded into other "anti-gravity" realms of extreme sports: BMX bicycles and "mountain boarding." And then the even more extreme sport of motocross, and motorcycle flights upside-down-no-hands back flips filmed from helicopters, over inconceivable distances.

Back home in Petaluma, I went back to my regular way of life: building projects all over the San Francisco Bay Area. When I had started working at Powell, I could tell it was going to be a photogenic couple of years. So I always had a good supply of film and as soon as I could afford it, I upgraded to a Canon SLR. I took thousands of photos during those skateboard years, and thereafter pictures of my travels and jobsites, and collected them into physical photo albums. I would pull them out to help tell my stories to whomever; sometimes as a visual resume for new clients, but most the time just to share what life had shown me to friends. I had quite a few of them by the year 2000 including the construction of the Gold Pyramid, the SkateZone, SkateStreet, the last hot tub I ever put together, Carol's stamped concrete driveway, overseas trips to Nepal, Bali, and Costa Rica and two projects that Doug Hechter connected me with: a lavish and tasteful mansion of recycled redwood and the installation of 400-year old doors in a newly created Santa Barbara villa; and a yurt on a mountainside in Big Sur.

For a project to commemorate the new century, I decided to learn how to make websites and put all my albums online. It's not that hard. I got a book on basic HTML, and an editing program that shows you how what you've coded will display on screen. I scanned some of those photographs I had in the albums and put them up online on my website. Check it out:

www.unclejohnsweb.com

Now that I've written this book, I've got about a thousand more photos that I could use to illustrate the stories. I am publishing the text as an Amazon print-on-demand paperback, and as a Kindle e-reader. These formats won't allow me to publish the quality and quantity of the photos I want. So my current plan is to put these photos up on a new website.

www.antigravitydevicecompany.com

Chapter 31 Making a Living

So what's the point of all this? My old friend the material question calls me awake. I've got to make a living. So I take a big breath and start doing the obvious steps of answering ads, sending résumés for anything I'm qualified for, getting the word of mouth moving. It's when I'm in that receptive, open-to-anything state of mind, a new venue for my skills comes into focus, a voice says, "OK, you're hired," and the stage is set for a whole new drama. That's the way it's always been for me.

I think the fact that I like having a job tilts the karmic odds in my favor. I like being down at the mine before anyone. I like being there early, drinking my coffee and reading the newspaper in the dawn while my co-workers straggle in. I like having some cooperative effort to occupy the day. I like having friends to have laughs with, projects to succeed at; I like lunch; I like going back to work; I like solving building problems; I like quitting time; I like working late when there's a reason to. I feel some pain and I leave a little blood on every job, and I even like that. When you love your work, turns out, all lunches are free, and the lumps are worth the price. Sometimes you end up in the hole; sometimes you got a pile left over. It's not about the gold; it's about digging what you're doing all day, and the treasure of discovering the characters that you're digging with.

What inhales, exhales. When the project is over, I'm ready for a new adventure. I like the finale too. The end of most projects goes like this: The boss or client comes up to you, says, in so many words, "Good job, now get out of here!" Your creation is completed; your tribe dissolves. Next time, roles may be reversed: I might be the foreman of a crew, or the general contractor, or just a carpenter on the team. I'd just as soon be a small player. The chief gets the big headdress and the big headaches.

JW has been working as the archivist and resident videographer at Skate One since 2002, converting the entire Powell-Peralta video library to digital video format. His first major projects were to do the DVD authoring of the company's original VHS videos for re-release and to create bonus features from the archive of never-before-seen footage. When he got full circle to The Search For Animal Chin, he included a screening of those same members of the Bones Brigade making comments and cracking each other up while watching the entire video.

When he had the project finished, JW drove up to see me at home in Petaluma. In an odd coincidence, it just so happened that Joel Watson appeared unexpectedly, the very same day. I have seen him just 3 times in the last 25 years. He lives in Missouri and just pops in on me when business brings him to Northern California. His visits are always hilarious, and this time the three of us watched the video of the Bones Brigade commenting while watching Animal Chin. I wish we had audio of our commentary over the top of theirs. That was 2005.

By 2010, Stacy and George had teamed up again to reissue the iconic Powell-Peralta skateboards from their heyday, and in 2011, Stacy went to work on a feature length documentary of the whole Bones Brigade phenomenon. He interviewed all the key figures in the saga. JW was enlisted to take behind the scenes shots of the interviews being taped and provide clips from Powell's vast archive of footage. When all 95 hours of interviews were all in the can, Stacy had all the dialogue transcribed into print. JW was tasked to locate the highlighted clips and put them together in a rough edit for Stacy and his L.A. editor.

I happened to be taking a two-year break from my Northern California adventures to take care of my 100-year old mother in her final days in Carpinteria, so I had a lot of spare time. JW's responsibilities got so huge that he set me up with the editing software, Final Cut Pro, so that I could do his overload of busy work for putting together the rough edit. In January 2012, Stacy's Bones Brigade: An Autobiography was screened for the first time at the Sundance Film Festival. JW was credited as one of the producers.

Somewhere JW got the idea to combine adventure with the material question of survival. And that's the point of all this. The need to make a living is a ticket to making a great life.

Do you need a job? What amazing good fortune.

Roll Out

You can probably tell the admiration I have for the courage and creativity of skaters.

Skateboarding has all the skill and danger of a martial art, but with no adversary; only gravity, physics and hard reality. Once understood, the adversaries are indispensible to the dance, aren't they? What a metaphor for existence.

To us folks who don't roll, a skater's frame of mind is available: Find a perfect wave in the everyday hardscape, or make one for yourself; find the good news of a foggy day, a friend in the material question, love and laughter in your job.

So there you go:

The Anti Gravity Device Company:

Elevating Skaters Since 1987.

Gone are: Vern Johnson, Ves Fowler, Moose Trapasso, Artie Corradi, Tim Garrety, Dick Latvala, Gary Crawford and Andrew Gordon. I miss all you characters I worked with, dead and alive. Did we not have fun?

.

— John Oliver, April 7, 2017

www.ingramcontent.com/pod-product-compliance
Lightning Source LLC
Chambersburg PA
CBHW051823040426
42447CB00006B/336

* 9 7 8 0 6 9 2 8 5 3 7 9 5 *